"Any poem that has worth expresses the whole life of the poet. It gives a view of what the poet is."

William Carlos Williams, *Paterson IV*

Published in 1954, *The Desert Music and Other Poems* contained some of the most accomplished and remarkable works of Williams' career as a poet. "The Desert Music" is perhaps the finest of this rich harvest. In his perceptive interpretation of this work, Sherman Paul gives us at once the biography of a poem, of a poet, and of the act of poetic invention. With full explications, he explores the central metaphor of Williams' art and strikes at the core of his message to the world.

Written after a disabling, nearly fatal stroke, "The Desert Music" represents a "crisis of survival," an attempt by the aging poet to avoid the easy death of his creative powers. For death (descent), as he always believed, must be a condition of rebirth (ascent). In "The Desert Music" the descent is into the landscape of memory, "into the ground of the self, which, only because it contains all that has gone before, can prove itself a fertile darkness sufficiently generative for art."

To some extent, every poem by Williams is an agony of self-realization, for to him poetry is an instrument with which to master one's world or environment. On

: : THE MUSIC OF SURVIVAL : :

University of Illinois Press :: Urbana Chicago London :: 1968

The
Music
of
Survival

..

A
BIOGRAPHY
OF A POEM BY
WILLIAM
CARLOS
WILLIAMS

..

by
Sherman
Paul

FOR BROOKSIE

. .
. .

Any poem that has worth expresses the whole life of the poet. It gives a view of what the poet is.

— Williams, *Paterson IV*.

. .
. .

— *Were you up here last night?*
Yes.
What were you doing?
Writing.
What did you write?
The story of my life —

— Williams, *The Autobiography*.

: : preface

Like the poem it treats, this essay has a biography, a brief one that can be told in terms of an incident and some acknowledgments of indebtedness.

The incident is of little significance to anyone but me; even I did not remember it until I began to write, and then, perhaps for the ironies it contained, I thought of it many times. In June, 1951, when William Carlos Williams delivered "The Desert Music" at Sanders Theatre in Cambridge, Massachusetts, I was not far away — in Warren House, just across Harvard Yard. I was busy working up my fall lectures on American literature, but Williams was terra incognita to me and I did not bother to attend. Eliot was familiar to me: I had seen him many times, at first mistaking him for a latter-day Emerson, walking through the parking lot between Warren House and the Faculty Club; and I knew his work and had heard him lecture and read his poems. Once I had almost been impaled on the fence at Memorial Hall by the pressing throng that had come to hear him, and, because of lack of space, had been seated with him on the stage of Sanders Theatre. I was to see him again and spend a memorable evening in his company. Year after year I taught some of his poems. But not Williams, who was neither sufficiently nor well represented in the anthologies and whom, again, I did not bother to dig up for myself.

I discovered the Williams of *In the American Grain* many years before I turned to the poet, and I turned to the poet only when James Kidder Guimond asked me to direct his dissertation on Williams. For engaging my attention and putting me to work, I am most indebted to him — and for the many kinds of assistance that only one so dedicated and expert in his subject can provide. And to an almost equal degree I am grateful and indebted to the students of my seminar for our joint exploration of Williams' considerable work. For them I first advanced the idea of this essay.

I owe much to Mrs. Florence H. Williams for permission to quote from her husband's work and to consult his manuscripts, to Mr. James Laughlin for negotiating with Mrs. Williams, to Mr. Donald Gallup and The Beinecke Rare Book and Manuscript Library of Yale University and to Mr. David Posner and the Lockwood Memorial Library of the State University of New York at Buffalo for making these manuscripts available to me, to Cid Corman for bibliographical aid and permission to quote from his letter to Williams, and to the Research Board and the Center for Advanced Study of the University of Illinois for material assistance.

The challenging readings of the manuscript of this essay by Warner Berthoff, James Guimond, William Rueckert, and Austin Warren are cherished debts of friendship and scholarship. I honor them here, along with the debts, equally cherished, I owe to Leonard F. Dean, Jack Stillinger, and G. M. Paul for steady encouragement.

The method of this essay is in some ways one of economy. In explicating the poem, as in treating the poet's biography, I have briefly considered, or perhaps merely located, some of the central issues of a new poetics; I did not think it necessary to elaborate and argue these issues — the work, certainly, of a larger, stricter undertaking. The method I have employed also has a biography. Perhaps I need only explain that I call this essay a biography because I subscribe to the good common sense of Eliot who, in *The Use of Poetry and the Use of Criticism,* said that we cannot "judge and enjoy a man's poetry while leaving wholly out of account all of the things for which he cared deeply, and on behalf of which he turned his poetry to account."

S.P.

::contents

:: one

It is not true, as William Carlos Williams says in *I Wanted to Write a Poem: The Autobiography of the Works of a Poet,* that the other poems in *The Desert Music* are more important than the title poem. They seemed so to him because in them he had consciously used his new measure, the variable foot. And they were, almost all of them, among the finest poems he had ever written — no other volume contains such a rich harvest of poetry. But "The Desert Music" is the longest and most accomplished of these remarkable poems on the themes closest to the life of the aging poet. Its theme is as insistent and profound as that of any of them; its complexity is greater; and its achievement is finer. Without openly admitting it, Williams acknowledged the importance of the poem by giving its title to the book.[1]

In his letters, Williams called the poem his " '15 minute' " poem.[2] It was one of the few poems that he had ever been requested to write or to deliver publicly. At the beginning of his career, he had read two poems at a public reading — perhaps at the Armory Show — and, in that time of artistic resurgence, had even gone to Chicago to read his poems in some artist's studio and before a press club.[3] Since then, especially in recent years, he had "performed" often, mostly before university audiences — in fact, the episode recalled in "The Desert Music" had occurred the previous autumn, in 1950, on his return from a triumphant tour of the West, the tour with whose account he concludes *The Autobiography,* the book that had almost killed him.

"It was from overwork on my *Autobiography,*" he told Marianne Moore, "that I went under. I might have died."[4] He had had an apoplectic stroke, not a second heart attack, and it had, he informed Robert Lowell, "disabled my right side and [for a time] knocked out my speech. . . ."[5] But having confronted him with the possibility of death, and of mental incapacity, which he said he feared more, it had had the effect of prompting him to clarify his purpose. Now he felt, as he explained to Louis Martz, that "I must gather together the stray ends of what I have been thinking and make my full statement as to their meaning[,] or quit." He was freed at last from the practice of medicine, and he had now "the opportunity to complete my task as a poet"— a task whose successful completion, however, seemed uncertain: "I hope the next few months can convince me that I can survive. . . ."[6]

One trial of the poet, an immediate challenge, came during his illness and at the time he was seeing to press the final portion of *The Autobiography.* This was an invitation to read a poem before the Phi Beta Kappa society of Harvard University, at its annual ceremonies in Sanders Theatre. He had no poem ready for the occasion, and the composition of the poem, which kept him busy for more than a month, exhausted him. But the invitation to read the poem meant much to him, not only because, as he told Martz, "I feel that many of my culminating ideas as to form have entered into this poem," but because in more than formal matters he knew that for him it was an "important event."[7]

With his crippled speech, Williams managed to read "The Desert Music" on June 18, 1951.

:: THE DESERT MUSIC

— the dance begins: to end about a form
propped motionless — on the bridge
between Juárez and El Paso — unrecognizable
in the semi-dark

       Wait!

The others waited while you inspected it,
on the very walk itself   .

       Is it alive?

           — neither a head,
legs nor arms!

     It isn't a sack of rags someone
has abandoned here   .   torpid against
the flange of the supporting girder   .   ?

       an inhuman shapelessness,
knees hugged tight up into the belly

    Egg-shaped!

         What a place to sleep!
on the International Boundary. Where else,
interjurisdictional, not to be disturbed?

How shall we get said what must be said?

Only the poem.

Only the counted poem, to an exact measure:
to imitate, not to copy nature, not
to copy nature

NOT, prostrate, to copy nature
                              but a dance! to dance
two and two with him —
                    sequestered there asleep,
                                    right end up!

        A music
supersedes his composure, hallooing to us
across a great distance   .   .

                              wakens the dance
who blows upon his benumbed fingers!

                              Only the poem
only the made poem, to get said what must
be said, not to copy nature, sticks
in our throats   .

The law? The law gives us nothing
but a corpse, wrapped in a dirty mantle.
The law is based on murder and confinement,
long delayed,
but this, following the insensate music,
is based on the dance:

                    an agony of self-realization
bound into a whole
by that which surrounds us   .

                    I cannot escape

I cannot vomit it up

Only the poem!

Only the made poem, the verb calls it
                              into being.

:: 4

— it looks too small for a man.
A woman. Or a very shriveled old man.
Maybe dead. They probably inspect the place
and will cart it away later   .

                    Heave it into the river.
A good thing.

Leaving California to return east, the fertile desert,
                    (were it to get water)
surrounded us, a music of survival, subdued, distant, half
                    heard; we were engulfed
by it as in the early evening, seeing the wind lift
                    and drive the sand, we
passed Yuma. All night long, heading for El Paso to
                    meet our friend,
we slept fitfully. Thinking of Paris, I waked to the tick
                    of the rails. The
jagged desert   .

                        — to tell
        what subsequently I saw and what heard

                          — to place myself (in
my nature) beside nature

                        — to imitate
nature (for to copy nature would be a
        shameful thing)

                  I lay myself down:

The Old Market's a good place to begin:
Let's cut through here —
                    tequila's only
a nickel a slug in these side streets.

Keep out though. Oh, it's all right at
this time of day but I saw H. terribly
beaten up in one of those joints. He
asked for it. I thought he was going to
be killed. I do
my drinking on the main drag   .

                              That's the bull ring
Oh, said Floss, after she got used to the
change of light   .
                              What color! Isn't it
wonderful!

            — paper flowers *(para los santos)*
baked red-clay utensils, daubed
with blue, silverware,
dried peppers, onions, print goods, children's
clothing   .   the place deserted all but
for a few Indians squatted in the
booths, unnoticing (don't you think it)
as though they slept there   .

            There's a second tier. Do you
want to go up?

            What makes Texans so tall?
We saw a woman this morning in a mink cape
six feet if she was an inch. What a woman!

Probably a Broadway figure.

— tell you what else we saw: about a million
sparrows screaming their heads off
in the trees of that small park where
the buses stop, sanctuary,
I suppose,
from the wind driving the sand in that way
about the city   .

:: 6

                    Texas rain they call it

— and those two alligators in the fountain   .

There were four

            I saw only two

                        They were looking
right at you all the time   .

Penny please! Give me penny please, mister.

                    Don't give them anything.

                        .   instinctively
one has already drawn one's naked
wrist away from those obscene fingers
as in the mind a vague apprehension speaks
and the music rouses   .

                        Let's get in here.
                    a music! cut off as
the bar door closes behind us.

                    We've got
another half hour.

                    — returned to the street,
the pressure moves from booth to booth along
the curb. Opposite, no less insistent
the better stores are wide open. Come in
and look around. You don't have to buy: hats,
riding boots, blankets   .

                    Look at the way,
slung from her neck with a shawl, that young
Indian woman carries her baby!

:: 7

                 — a stream of Spanish,
as she brushes by, intense, wide-
eyed in eager talk with her boy husband

— three half-grown girls, one of them eating a
pomegranate. Laughing.

                       and the serious tourist,
man and wife, middle-aged, middle-western,
their arms loaded with loot, whispering
together — still looking for bargains   .

                       and the aniline
red and green candy at the little booth
tended by the old Indian woman.
           Do you suppose anyone actually
buys — and eats the stuff?

My feet are beginning to ache me.

                  We still got a few minutes.
Let's try here. They had the mayor
up last month for taking $3000 a week from
the whorehouses of the city. Not much left
for the girls. There's a show on.

                 Only a few tables
occupied. A conventional orchestra — this
place livens up later — playing the usual local
jing-a-jing — a boy and girl team, she
                      confidential with someone
off stage. Laughing: just finishing the act.

So we drink until the next turn — a strip tease.

Do you mean it? Wow! Look at her.

                  You'd have to be
pretty drunk to get any kick out of that.

She's no Mexican. Some worn-out trouper from
the States. Look at those breasts

There is a fascination
seeing her shake
the beaded sequins from
a string about her hips

She gyrates but it's
not what you think,
one does not laugh
to watch her belly.

One is moved but not
at the dull show. The
guitarist yawns. She
cannot even sing. She

has about her painted
hardihood a screen
of pretty doves which
flutter their wings.

Her cold eyes perfunc-
torily moan but do not
smile. Yet they bill
and coo by grace of
a certain candor. She

is heavy on her feet.
That's good. She
bends forward leaning
on the table of the
balding man sitting
upright, alone, so that
everything hangs for-
ward.
            What the hell

are you grinning
to yourself about? Not
at *her?*
   The music!
I like her. She fits

the music .

Why don't these Indians get over this nauseating
prattle about their souls and their loves and sing
us something else for a change?

This place is rank
with it. She
at least knows she's
part of another tune,
knows her customers,
has the same
opinion of them as I
have. That gives her
one up . one up
following the lying
music .

There is another music. The bright-colored candy
of her nakedness lifts her unexpectedly
to partake of its tune .

        Andromeda of those rocks,
the virgin of her mind   .   those unearthly
greens and reds
         in her mockery of virtue
she becomes unaccountably virtuous .
       though she in no
way pretends it .

Let's get out of this.

:: 10

                    In the street it hit
me in the face as we started to walk again. Or
am I merely playing the poet? Do I merely invent
it out of whole cloth? I thought   .

              What in the form of an old whore in
              a cheap Mexican joint in Juárez, her bare
              can waggling crazily can be
              so refreshing to me, raise to my ear
              so sweet a tune, built of such slime?

              Here we are. They'll be along any minute.
              The bar is at the right of the entrance,
              a few tables opposite which you have to pass
              to get to the dining room, beyond.

              A foursome, two oversize Americans, no
              longer young, got up as cowboys,
              hats and all, are drunk and carrying on
              with their gals, drunk also,

              especially one inciting her man, the
              biggest, *Yip ee!* to dance in
              the narrow space, oblivious to everything
              — she is insatiable and he is trying

              stumblingly to keep up with her.
              Give it the gun, pardner! *Yip ee!* We
              pushed by them to our table, seven
              of us. Seated about the room

              were quiet family groups, some with
              children, eating. Rather a better
              class than you notice
              on the streets. So here we are. You

              can see through into the kitchen
              where one of the cooks, his shirt sleeves

rolled up, an apron over
the well-pressed pants of a street

suit, black hair neatly parted,
a tall
good-looking man, is working
absorbed, before a chopping block

Old fashioneds all around?

So this is William
Carlos Williams, the poet   .

Floss and I had half consumed
our quartered hearts of lettuce before
we noticed the others hadn't touched theirs   .
You seem quite normal. Can you tell me? Why
does one want to write a poem?

Because it's there to be written.

Oh. A matter of inspiration then?

Of necessity.

Oh. But what sets it off?

I am that he whose brains
are scattered
aimlessly

— and so,
the hour done, the quail eaten, we were on
our way back to El Paso.

Good night. Good
night and thank you . No. Thank you. We're
going to walk   .

— and so, on the naked wrist, we feel again
those insistent fingers   .

                              Penny please, mister.
Penny please. Give me penny.

                              Here! now go away.

— but the music, the music has reawakened
as we leave the busier parts of the street
and come again to the bridge in the semi-dark,
pay our fee and begin again to cross   .
seeing the lights along the mountain back of El
Paso and pause to watch the boys calling out
to us to throw more coins to them standing
in the shallow water   .   so that's
where the incentive lay, with the annoyance
of those surprising fingers.

                              So you're a poet?
a good thing to be got rid of — half drunk,
a free dinner under your belt, even though you
get typhoid — and to have met people you
can at least talk to   .

                    relief from that changeless, endless
inescapable and insistent music   .

                    What else, Latins, do you yourselves
seek but relief!
with the expressionless ding dong you dish up
to us of your souls and your loves, which
we swallow. Spaniards! (though these are mostly
Indians who chase the white bastards
through the streets on their Independence Day
and try to kill them)   .

                              What's that?

Oh, come on.

But what's THAT?

the music! the
music! as when Casals struck
and held a deep cello tone
and I am speechless   .

There it sat
in the projecting angle of the bridge flange
as I stood aghast and looked at it —
in the half-light: shapeless or rather returned
to its original shape, armless, legless,
headless, packed like the pit of a fruit into
that obscure corner — or
a fish to swim against the stream — or
a child in the womb prepared to imitate life,
warding its life against
a birth of awful promise. The music
guards it, a mucus, a film that surrounds it,
a benumbing ink that stains the
sea of our minds — to hold us off — shed
of a shape close as it can get to no shape,
a music! a protecting music   .

I *am* a poet! I
am. I am. I am a poet, I reaffirmed, ashamed

Now the music volleys through as in
a lonely moment I hear it. Now it is all
about me. The dance! The verb detaches itself
seeking to become articulate   .

And I could not help thinking
of the wonders of the brain that
hears that music and of our
skill sometimes to record it.

The performance amused Williams, for some of "the gentlemen sitting on the platform" were not delighted, as were the students, by his "shocking poem" — "I think they must have fumigated Memorial Hall after I left."[8] To mention the whores of Juárez introduced the kind of superficial "anti-poetic" material that had always distressed the genteel and the purists of poetry. Even Princess Marguerite Caetani, who accepted the poem for her respectably avant garde *Botteghe Oscure,* insisted that in the phrase "her bare/can waggling crazily" he change "can" to "buttocks"[9] — a change of little formal and no thematic importance that Williams consented to make and amended when *The Desert Music and Other Poems* was published in 1954.

:: two

Williams introduces his comments on *The Desert Music* by noting that "there is something special about this book." This special aspect, only partially explained by his remarks on the place of the title poem in his formal development and public regard as a poet, is pointed to, when linking the poem to his illness, he tells Edith Heal, several years afterward, "I had just returned from a trip to the West and the picture of the desert country around El Paso was fresh in my mind. I'd crossed the desert and *seen* the desert."[1] He had been West before, in the summer of 1947, and had seen the desert then — he had visited Taos with Robert McAlmon.[2] But because it had not touched his life, that trip had not significantly informed his poetry, where the more recent trip had. "It is always important to me," he adds in the same interview, "to be familiar with what I am writing about" — and in writing "The Desert Music" he was. He had *seen* the desert but only because, subsequently, he had seen death, and that — he is still relieved to remember — was the desert he had crossed.

He had not written the poem on his return but at a time when he had no poem to read and it was necessary — it is a burden of "The Desert Music" — to reaffirm his poetic vocation by avoiding the easy death of his creative powers, the death referred to in a poem of that name:

So this is death that I
refuse to rouse and write
but prefer to lie here
half asleep with a mind

not aflame but merely
flickering lacking breath
to fan it — from
the comfortable dark womb[3]

He had, in fact, searched at the portal of the dark womb
of his own past in the months preceding the occasion of
the poem. He had written *The Autobiography,* a termi-
nal and satisfying book beyond which he needn't go.
His *Collected Later Poems* were published in 1950, the
Collected Earlier Poems in 1951, and the long composition of *Paterson,* as originally projected, was also over;
and like the poet in its fourth book ("Shh! the old man's
asleep") he might, having bequeathed his poetic mission
to a younger generation, quietly give up. From this
dream of retirement the stroke of death awakened him,
and saved him. For death (descent), as he always believed, was a condition of rebirth (ascent); and one feels
its psychic necessity, the necessity of the destructive blow
prefigured in the conjunction of violent death-and-birth
at the close of *Paterson IV*. Stricken, he was now able to
see that in writing *The Autobiography* he had too easily
crossed the desert of his own life and that his satisfaction
with it was a form of death. *The Autobiography* ends
with a full account of his western tour and a brief chapter on *Paterson,* and because of this juxtaposition the
triumph of the one is associated with the other. But now,
as "The Desert Music" shows, he was returning East,
coming back to some truths he had glossed over.

As always before, the comfort of the dark womb
yielded to the terror of self-confrontation and the terrible

agony of self-regeneration; and, as always, yet never with complete assurance of its efficacy because it was a temporal act, the act of creating poetry delivered him, "released" him. "The Desert Music" is a poem enacting such "agony of self-realization," a poem equal in power, though different in many ways, to another great poem on this theme, "Portrait of the Author"— which Robert McAlmon, incidentally, had once kept him from destroying.[4] In this early poem the advent of new life in spring tests the poet's resources for renewal; it is a seasonal crisis of spirit, such as Thoreau knew, and is treated in many of Williams' "nature" poems, usually with less intensity and disclosure of its wonderful terror. In the moment of terror, Williams writes:

> I am shaken, broken against a might
> that splits comfort, blows apart my
> careful partitions, crushes my house
> and leaves me — with shrinking heart
> and startled, empty eyes — peering out
> into a cold world.[5]

Both poems relate an experience whose meaning is most fully contemplated by Williams in "Night," a chapter of *A Voyage to Pagany* (1928), an autobiographical fiction of an earlier crisis in his career. This chapter, about his wanderings in Genoa, has no geographical warrant; it is set in Genoa in order to link the poet's disorientation on his "voyage," a return to pagan sources both historical and psychic, with Columbus' uncertainties about his voyage of discovery. The novel is a voyage of discovery, and the poet's disorientation is of a kind related to Columbus' that fittingly ends with his rediscovery of America. (Many years later, in keeping with this central metaphor of his work, Williams wrote concerning invention and measure: "We are nosing along a mysterious coast-line and have not yet broached the continent.")[6] The experience is comparable to that of Sam Houston described in the chapter "Descent" in *In the American Grain,* a book that Williams was working on during his travels in Europe in 1924. Houston, he writes, went to Europe "to see a strange New World," and in the crises of his life courageously "took the descent once more, to the ground," went back to the "beginning." The poet of *A Voyage to Pagany,* sighting the American shore on his return, concludes the book by saying, "So this is the beginning."

The poet, in Genoa, loses himself searching for the harbor at night and is overcome by a "nameless panic" and state of dreadful hallucinated somnolence. He imagines himself dead and, waking, "sense[s] vividly with open eyes the formlessness which terrified him asleep." He feels "the terror of emptiness . . . the terror of no form, the poet's ache." Meditating on this experience and its relation to art, he realizes that night is "the mother stuff" and artwork "a form of the night." Darkness and despair, he declares, are his home: "Here I have always retreated when I was beaten, to lie and breed with myself." And night becomes "sacred" to him, a sacred stuff and time, the body of the poet ("It is ourselves. — And he felt that his body extended to the horizon") and the time of love ("It is the generative hour. Of this I am made").[7]

Yet he recognizes another aspect of night — and another cause of terror — not so readily overcome by, and concurrent with, the act of self-generation: its otherness, its separateness. "The night is the body of someone else," he says. "Into which we have come." It is not necessarily coextensive with the self, though the self is wholly involved with it. Instead it is the circumstances of the self, its environment, which poetic invention — formal means at once sexual and exploratory — enables him to enter.[8]

"The birth of the imagination is like waking from a nightmare," Williams wrote in "Prologue to *Kora in Hell.*" "Never does the night seem so beneficent."[9] For waking frees the imagination for the dance (the dance of life), the complex movement relating poet to thing, self to world, that requires, always, its unique measure. The poem itself is an action of the imagination in its initiation or "entering into." This explains why formal invention, apart from its supreme cultural importance, means so much to Williams: with its help he develops and pursues the exploring self. And this also explains why his poetic quest figures as "a dream of love," as an endless sexual pursuit of "Beautiful Thing." *"The poet transforms himself into a satyr,"* he wrote, at the start, in *Kora in Hell, "and goes in pursuit of a white skinned dryad."*[10]

In *A Voyage to Pagany* this pursuit is most satisfactorily rendered in the protagonist's relations with Grace Black, the character in the novel who represents the pagan body of America. She is a contemporary Pocahontas, and as a result of his love affair with her, which he speaks of as "going forward . . . into a virgin continent," he experiences "clarity":

. . . he seemed to be sinking back through imprisoning circles of dark light as through the center of a flower, back to some dimly remembered past, Indian games — mad escapades. Back, back to a lost grace — his own early instincts, perfect and beautiful. Scale after scale dropped from him — more than he had known it to happen under any previous condition in his life before. He never felt less voluptuous, but clarified through and through, not the mind, not the spirit — but the whole body — clear, clear, clear as if he were made of some fine material strong yet permeable to every sense — opening, loosening, letting in the light.[11]

Williams' first major crisis and descent was commemorated in "The Wanderer," a long poem published originally in *The Egoist* in 1914 (along with work by Joyce and Pound) and used later as the initial poem of his collected poems. The crisis here, precipitated by the Paterson strike of 1912, involves the acceptance of his environment and is overcome by means of a ritual marriage and baptismal death in the "filthy Passaic."

His second crisis was the one of allegiance treated in *A Voyage to Pagany* (1928). In this book, the poet's disorientation expresses his actual confusion about America in another book, *The Great American Novel* (1923), where, amid the overwhelming welter of things, he fails to "work in," to find a way to begin, and to bring America to form. He may assert his ardent Americanism — call himself a "United Stateser"— yet it seems that as a result of this failure he was drawn to the Europe to which so many of his friends had gone. Momentarily — his sabbatical year from medicine was in part a sabbatical from America — he was willing to "run out," as he says in *Paterson I,* where once again, later in life, he faced a similar problem of ordering the ugly chaos of America. Of the poet Paterson, he says:

> he envies the men that ran
> and could run off
> toward the peripheries —
> to other centers, direct —
> for clarity (if
> they found it)
>   loveliness and
> authority in the world —[12]

This crisis, represented in the novel by the rootlessness of travel and the irresolution of sexual relationships, was resolved by the work of still another book of this time, *In the American Grain* (1925). Here the descent is historical, into the American past, and gives him ground of his own to stand on. This is the meaning of the experience of possession and clarity related in *A Voyage to Pagany* in the episodes concerned with Grace Black, to whom the poet gives "for a keepsake a copy of a book he had once published upon some characters from the American History."[13] As her name implies, Grace Black is both the dark and the light, the descent-enabling-ascent, the mysterious darkness which yields the poet light.

Now, in "The Desert Music," the culmination of a third major crisis, the descent is into memory, into the ground of the self, which, only because it contains all that has gone before, can prove itself a fertile darkness sufficiently generative for art. The self is always involved in renewal, but only now, in this crisis of survival, can it be said to breed with itself.[14]

To some extent every poem of Williams is an agony of self-realization because for him poetry is an action that mediates and sustains the self in the world. A poem is to him what an idea is to John Dewey, an instrument with which to master one's world, or environment. But the agony of "The Desert Music" — and it is important that it is the primary theme of the poem — is special because it occurs, as Williams intimated, at a crucial time in his career. On the successful composition of this poem he staked his survival as a poet. Its success confirmed his faith in the resources of the self and in its renewal by art, and it made possible the resplendent creation of the last years of his life. How the desert places yielded under the continuing act of poetry set free by this poem! What vindication of faith and verification of art, these last poems rising out of the dying ground!

"The Desert Music" affirmed survival through art, the great theme of Williams' last work, and opened, in a way *The Autobiography* had not, the landscape of memory. For the poet, limited in range of contact by illness, turned now to memory, turned back on himself in a manner similar to the pursuit of imagination by imagination — the hunt of the unicorn — in *Paterson V*.[15] This reflexiveness takes the form of reflectiveness, of meditation, which is the interior mode of much of the later poetry; and it explains the significance of Williams' use of "The Descent," originally a portion of *Paterson II*, and "The Desert Music" to enclose his new poems. "The Descent" belongs with the "The Desert Music" because the poet, in the daring descent of the latter poem, had learned — made good — the truth of the former:

> The descent beckons
>   as the ascent beckoned.
>   Memory is a kind
> of accomplishment,
>   a sort of renewal
>   even
> an initiation, since the spaces it opens are new places

And memory compensates for defeat and restores, unblemished, the Beautiful Thing, the object projected by and pursued by the imagination:

>   since
> the world it opens is always a place
>   formerly
>   unsuspected. A
> world lost,
>   a world unsuspected,
>   beckons to new places
> and no whiteness (lost) is so white as the memory
> of whiteness   .

Williams used this poem not, presumably, to introduce these themes, which are more appropriate to *The Desert Music* than to *Paterson II,* but because in it he had discovered, as he told Edith Heal, "my final conception of what my own poetry should be. . . ."[16] But the variable foot, for all of its importance and usefulness to him, is primarily a device for opening the line to the new cadences and continuities and spaciousness of thought. With it Williams entered a world where the imagination was supreme, and he discovered it at a time when he was beginning to feel the need for autobiographical expression.

:: three

The impulse to autobiography is not necessarily an impulse to confession, nor is it necessarily connected with the use of autobiographical materials in art. All of Williams' work, as he insists (and as a character in *Many Loves* reprovingly warns us), is an attempt to release the self:

> To break the walls and let him out.
> To escape, to write, to realize,
> to come through the obscurity
> of his surroundings to the flame —
> of himself. . . .[1]

He wanted, he says in *The Autobiography* where he also remarks that he has hidden it, to tell openly the secret of his life.[2]

His art involves the interaction of self and world and so by its very nature is "autobiographical" — and useful in telling his story. Of this interaction, the practice of medicine had been the essential means. "As a writer, I have been a physician, and as a physician a writer" — his callings are inextricable, one enabling the other.[3] Medicine gave him the stake in the world of affairs that saved him from the chaos of *la vie boheme* (not that the world of affairs wasn't chaotic), and what it took from him in time it repaid in literary independence, materials, and direct approach. As much as place, it secured the integrity of his life. But when he says that as a writer he has been a physician he means also that as a writer he has been a healer, performing the priestly function he approved in Joyce; and when he says that as a physician he has been a writer, he means not only that in his practice he has been attentive to the needs of the soul (the point of the story "Mind and Body") but that this has been his practice.[4] "My 'medicine,'" he explains in *The Autobiography,* setting it off to suggest its magical powers and to remind us of a medicine man like Doc Rivers, "— my 'medicine' was the thing which gained me entrance to the secret gardens of the self." And of this garden, where he sometimes discovers the evanescent Beautiful Thing ("the thing, in all its greatest beauty"), he adds, establishing the significant allusion to Columbus, "It lay there, another world, in the self."[5]

Williams entered that garden not by turning inward but by turning outward. Like Emerson, he was reluctant to look directly into the self, to know it introspectively, subjectively. Instead, he preferred to know it objectively, in the objects of the world and in his dance with its persons, places, and things. That his poems are objective (that is, objects in themselves) and momentary arrests of the swirl of life does not invalidate their correspondential function. For a poem, he believed, is both the "fixation by the imagination of the external as well as internal means of expression. . . ."[6] Yet even such poems, he found, could be "small and tied and gasping," a kind of "soliloquy without the 'living' in the world"; and other forms were often more satisfactory — the story or, better still, the play in which he identified with the characters and lived in the world.[7]

These forms of self-exploration are not autobiography. They are not prompted by the autobiographical impulse, which usually arises in a late stage of life when one is concerned more for the continuity than the topography of the self. Autobiography is born of time and concerns time, the time of the self, which is a vital quality of its inward experience and coherence; and one turns to it because the significance of one's life may be found within its "field," in the experiences that constitute one's relations to life. In Williams' career one begins to recognize the emergence of this impulse when time replaces space as the primary dimension in the organization of his work (as in *Paterson,* which should be compared with *The Great American Novel,* an earlier unsuccessful spatial treatment of similar materials); when sound replaces light as the agency of affirmation — when the poet begins to hear the music of memory and responds to the "hum of [the] valvèd voice" (as in "The Desert Music" in contrast to *A Voyage to Pagany*); and when the measure of his verse begins to answer to a new time, the time of memory (as in "The Descent" of *Paterson II*).

Such changes are not uniformly present or permanent in Williams' later work, but nevertheless they are profoundly radical and mark this watershed of his life. When almost fifty years old (in 1932), he told Marsden Hartley that he looked forward "to twenty years of continued development . . . with time for summations and reminiscences after that." In 1934, he told a correspondent that "autobiography doesn't mean a thing to me"; and he was not ready to undertake one in 1938, when he said that it would have "to come about in the manner of the seasons."[8] Yet the time for beginning his summations and reminiscences was nearer than he knew.

Its public advent was World War II, its private advent the death, in 1943, of Marsden Hartley, one of the first of his generation of artists to succumb. Williams' response to Hartley's death was angry and self-admonishing, for the brief obituary in the New York *Times* — the nothingness to which death seemed to have reduced Hartley's accomplishment — dismayed him, and he could not forgive Hartley for being overcome by fear of life. "Most of us need the very thing we never ask for," he told McAlmon. "What we need is some frank thinking and a few revolutions in our own guts; to hell with most of the sons of bitches that I know and myself along with them if I don't take hold of myself and turn about when I need to — or go ahead further if that's the game."[9]

As for the war, which involved his sons and intensified his medical work, it may be considered the equivalent in his experience of the Civil War in Whitman's. The title of the only book of poems he published during the war years indicates its significance: the war entered his life as a "wedge," introduced the violence, transformation, and cataclysmic birth, which, modulated by gentleness, are the dominant themes of these poems; it was a turning point that enabled him to go further. By taking his sons away from home, the war hastened their independence; and in letters to William Eric, the elder, he was now able to explain himself. ("I wrote because to maintain myself in a world much of which I didn't love I had to fight to keep myself as I wanted to be. The poems are me, in much of the faulty perspective in which I have existed in my own sight. . . .") During these years he became a grandfather ("Jinny came through it all right so there starts another generation . . .");[10] this not only confirmed the faith in on-going life expressed in *The Wedge* but probably contributed to its autumnal mood — to the willingness he expressed to "give up my job and join/the old men. . . ." Williams acknowledged the place of *The Wedge* in his development by using it to introduce *The Collected Later Poems,* but this decision was hardly valetudinarian, and asserted his determination to go ahead with his work. In the opening poem he calls for composition and invention and takes as his own the saxifrage, the "flower that splits/the rocks."[11]

The violence of his determination was the result of a poet's need to salvage something from the wreckage of war and also of the challenge that Eliot and Pound had presented him. By 1943, *Paterson,* that "impossible poem," was underway, and was intended, Williams told James Laughlin, to "assault . . . the cults and the kind of thought that destroyed Pound and made what it has made of Eliot."[12]

During these years Pound's wartime behavior deeply troubled Williams. (Pound was arrested for treason in Genoa in May, 1945, was flown to Washington to stand trial but was declared mentally unfit and sent to St. Elizabeth's Hospital in 1946.) He found it increasingly difficult to justify Pound's "stupidities" on the grounds of his importance as a poet. In his fullest comments on Pound, made at the time of the approaching trial, he did not exonerate Pound but explained his stupidities in such a way that it was possible to ask for leniency. His most significant comment, linking Pound and Henry James, concerned expatriation: "Ezra is one of a well recognized group of Americans who can't take the democratic virus and stand up under it, very distinguished men most of them who owe their distinction largely to their American origins."[13] This public statement generalized a more personal criticism of Pound's achievement, that he had "never really faced the job of putting his talents on a contemporary basis. . . ."[14] Williams, of course, had faced this difficulty and hoped now to overcome it. He had told Laughlin in 1940, ". . . my perceptions overtook him [Pound] twenty years ago — not however my accomplishment. When I have finished, if I can go on to the finish, there'll be another measuring."[15]

Pound never troubled Williams in the unsettling way Eliot did, and Eliot troubled him now by raising again in an article in *Partisan Review* — and being seriously attended to for it — the issue of culture which was a central preoccupation of Williams' life and his immediate concern in *Paterson*.[16] More than anything else this put him on trial as a poet and forced him to consider his past achievement.

From the time of "The Wanderer," the poem that had replaced his Keatsian poem about an abducted prince who had awakened to find himself without country, bride (Beautiful Thing), language, or past, Williams, more than any poet of his generation, had struck up for the New World — and a new culture.[17] In his work he had tried to discover these missing things — in all, to use a phrase of Frank Lloyd Wright's that appears in the introduction to *The Wedge*, to find the form (an open form) that fitted "the nature of his materials. . . ."[18] As he wrote in 1934 in "The American Background," his most brilliant statement on culture, he hoped by contact with American materials to create a "culture of immediate references," a culture as "locally related" as a plant in the earth. This was the kind of primary culture — not a secondary or borrowed culture — that he believed was needed: a living culture realizing "the qualities of a place in relation to the life which occupies it; embracing everything involved, climate, geographic position, relative size, history, other cultures [Williams was never chauvinistic] — as well as the character of its sands, flowers, minerals and the condition of knowledge within its borders." Such a culture was living because it was being built "from the ground up" and was not the thing created (Culture: an artifact) so much as the act of creating (culture: a process); it was, as Wright said of true art and culture, an "indigenous growth." And it was characterized for Williams by an essential power of the imagination — the "act of lifting these things into an ordered and utilized whole. . . ." He had always maintained that poetry involved such an action and discovered "an order . . . in its living character of today," and this was the conception of vital interior order that he had in mind when he told Laughlin of his work on *Paterson* and his hostility to Pound and Eliot.[19] In his sense of the meaning of culture, he would try to be what his rivals in their ways had tried to be: a poet of culture.[20]

The difficult formal problems arising from the inseparable nature of culture and form that Williams himself was facing were, he told Horace Gregory, the very things that Pound and Eliot had avoided, and that was why he felt that both poets had "slipped back, intellectually, from their early promise." Eliot, moreover, in writing of culture — and especially of local culture — treated ideas which were already well known (Williams traced them to John Dewey a generation earlier) but which he had never tested as a poet. "He fled the rigors of an American application," Williams said, "embracing the Church largely to cover up that." He did not understand the relation of local to general culture: that (in the structural imagery of *Paterson*) the "flow must originate from the local to the general as a river to the sea and then back to the local from the sea in rain." Nor was he "the agent and the maker" of culture because he was not a poet who lived "on the location"— who "lives locally, and whose senses are applied no way else than locally to particulars. . . ."[21]

Williams' arraignment of Eliot was of long standing and its vehemence characteristic of the open, personal literary quarrels of the 1920's. (In "Prologue to *Kora in*

Hell," where he judged his contemporaries, he marked down Eliot as a "subtle conformist.")[22] Now, however, his views seemed to him to be vindicated by *Paterson I* (1946), whose favorable reception was the beginning of a steadily increasing reputation. The notice of two young poets, Robert Lowell and Randall Jarrell, especially pleased him. Lowell wrote in *Sewanee Review* that "in *Paterson* his position has paid off, when compared to Pound's. It is a sort of anti-Cantos rooted in America. . . ." He avoided comparing Williams with Eliot, Stevens, Tate, or Auden, mentioning only the superiority of his poem to *The Bridge,* but he said that "for experience and observation, it has . . . a richness that makes almost all other contemporary poetry look a little second-hand," and he predicted that, if what remained to be written was as good, *"Paterson* will be the most successful really long poem since *The Prelude.*"[23] Jarrell, whose review Lowell believed would become famous as an example of "the shock of recognition," discerned the "musical" (both spatial and temporal) organization of the poem, said that there had never been "a poem more American," and predicted, conditionally, that "the whole poem will be the best very long poem that any American has written."[24]

This was a season of praise, for the University of Buffalo, where Williams had begun to deposit his papers, awarded him an honorary degree in 1946, the *Briarcliff Quarterly* devoted an issue to him, and the *Quarterly Review of Literature* printed the largest group of poems he had ever had published at "one showing."[25] Yet fitting as the favorable recognition was in one sense, it was disturbing in another because it came at a crucial time in the history of poetry — at the time when the notion of poet of culture, so important to a generation of poets, was being tried in the prosecution of Ezra Pound. Pound's "trial" was the *cause célèbre* of poetry in our time, and in the essays written in Pound's defense Williams found much that shaped the conception of his *Autobiography* and the subsequent books of *Paterson* — and much that fed the autobiographical impulse at work in both.

Probably of greatest significance was another essay by Eliot, the one in Pound's behalf in *Poetry* to which Williams referred in a letter to Pound at St. Elizabeth's.[26] What is impressive here are Eliot's strategy of defense and his measures of achievement. Eliot waived the ultimate issue of Pound's greatness and even the contemporary issue of his genuineness for "a third kind of judgment which may be passed upon him in his later years, the material for which is not only his poetry, but the principle of writing which he has exemplified and defended." Choosing to show "the things for which a man like Pound has stood, in his own time," Eliot went back to the situation in poetry in the years 1915-32, and treating Pound as if he were dead, wrote a eulogy of his accomplishments. Pound may have shown "a kind of resistance against growing into any environment" (in the same issue of *Poetry*, George Dillon spoke of Pound as "the expatriate *sub specie aeternitatis*") but he had been an exemplary teacher of the younger men, an admirable judge of poetry, and an advocate whose devotion to the art of poetry was equaled only by Valéry and, perhaps, by Yeats.[27]

At this very time, Williams himself was writing about Pound in "Letter to an Australian Editor" — about his present dilemma, his genius, the debt he owed him, but chiefly about their fundamental opposition over "the genesis of poetic genius," a difference between them that for a long time had been represented by Williams' preference for bread and Pound's for caviar.[28] This letter, printed in the issue of the *Briarcliff Quarterly* honoring him, is perhaps the best and most succinct statement, among many, of Williams' rationale for poetry. Pound is its occasion, the pivot on which it turns, the prototypal poet in respect to his indifference to environment, the very matrix, for Williams, of art. Williams likens Pound's mind to a "bird bred of air without female or . . . nest of any sort"; he is a poet developed "androgynetically from the past itself mind to mind," not, as Williams considered himself to be, from direct engagement with "the supplying female," the present surging immediate life. This difference is crucial, for the "direct approach" insures the nurture that the androgynous eventually fails to provide; it feeds the very life of the poet and his forms: "not only his fertility but those forms themselves — arise from the society about him of which he is (if he is to be fed) a part. . . ." Nurtured in this way, the poet is democratic, truly a *representative man* sustained by and sustaining a living society, an agent of its culture, where the poet, like Pound, who clings to the forms of the past (Culture), finds nothing in the present and wishes "for political, social and economic autocracy."[29]

Inevitably *Paterson,* which was intended to crown a lifetime's work, reflected these matters. It is about a poet in his own time who feels responsible for culture and considers poetry a means of its redemption;[30] a poet who is familiar with the ideas of social credit and rails against the economic legacy of Alexander Hamilton, and whose rages over the low state of American culture are incendiary if not treasonous. Though offering disagreements with Pound, especially over the nature of culture and the nature of poetry, the poem honors him to the extent that it incorporates his views and makes plausible his profound cultural discontent.[31] For in spite of Williams' commitment to the local, the poet in *Paterson* is divorced from his world — in a psychological sense, expatriated. Living on location has not insured his success as an agent and maker of culture; and except for the encouragement he has given the younger men (the instance in the poem is Allen Ginsberg) he has failed, grown old, and abdicated his purpose.[32] He has not become the hero of culture one might have anticipated from the splendid response to *Paterson I,* the first book of his history, just an old man who, while warning against the terrible sea of death, has himself begun to live in memory. Williams once denied that Prufrock was "a New World type," yet his initial conception of the poet in *Paterson* is of a genteel man of letters not unlike Prufrock, and the poem he has fashioned —"this dream of/the whole poem"— is a dream of cultural fulfillment whose realization seems impossible when the poet wakens to the violence of our time.[33]

The failure of the poet in *Paterson* may have been an outcome of the structure of the poem. Both the life of the poet in the poem and the flow of history in his mind follow the course of the seasons from springtime to winter; like the river that runs through the poem, the movement is deathward, from undefiled sources to the bloody sea. The poem, even with its cyclical guarantee of renewal, is more desolate than *The Waste Land,* for beyond the impaired fertility of woman and nature the only hope it offers resides in the power of the inventive mind — in the power of man-the-maker, the poet, who in the account of this poem is not strong enough to stand alone against the tides of history, the "political, social and economic maelstrom" that in the *Briarcliff Quarterly* letter Williams said the poet should ride.[34]

That the poet in the poem, after his brave start, seems too quickly to be overtaken by old age and never gets beyond the stage of acceptance of "The Wanderer" is perhaps the outcome not wholly of the poem's design but of events current with its composition. Early in February, 1948, Williams suffered a heart attack and his first overwhelming apprehension of death — there is a curious prefigurement in *A Dream of Love,* published in this year, in which a doctor-poet succumbs in mid-career to a heart attack when about to possess Beautiful Thing.[35] At this time ("Only yesterday, lying ill here in bed at the age of 64") he began the autobiographical notes published in *Poetry.*[36] He was, and had been, preoccupied with death, his own and that of his aged mother, with whom he closely identified. She died in 1949, and occasioned the comment ("What the devil are we alive for? To hide ourselves?") that set in motion the foreword to *The Autobiography.*[37] Old age and death are among the themes of *The Clouds,* published in 1948; he wishes to be "appeased against/this dryness and the death implied"; in the fashion of Emily Dickinson he writes of "The day before I died"; and in "The Woodpecker," he is concerned that "From a height we fall, innocent,/to our deaths."[38] In 1949, when on the publication of *Paterson III* he explained his intentions, he said that "The course of the river . . . seemed more and more to resemble my own life as I more and more thought of it" and he described the theme of the poem as "a searching for the redeeming language by which a man's premature death . . . might have been prevented."[39]

Then there was an anticlimax of critical praise. Enthusiasm for *Paterson* waned with each new installment, a response that may be characterized most sharply by Randall Jarrell's review of the completed poem. For the older poet the pain of this review was increased by its deadly reminiscent personal manner. *"Paterson (Book I),"* Jarrell recalled, "seemed to me a wonderful poem. . . ." Then: "I waited for the next three books of *Paterson* more or less as you wait for someone who has gone to break the bank at Monte Carlo for the second, third, and fourth times; I was afraid that I knew what was going to happen, but I kept wishing as hard as I could that it wouldn't." His conclusion now is that Williams' luck ran out, that the poem was not a formal success and had "been getting rather steadily worse" — "Book IV is so disappointing that I do not want to write about it at any length. . . ." Williams, instead of surpassing Pound, had himself adopted a Pound-like "Organization of Irrelevance (or, perhaps the Irrelevance of Organization)": ". . . all three later books are worse organized, more eccentric and idiosyncratic, more self-indulgent, than the first," and the poetry of the poem had diminished. To all of this hard criticism, Jarrell added a capital summary: that Williams, having been "the last of the good poets of his generation to become properly appreciated," had been overvalued; that he was a *"very* limited poet" by nature (he "is not, of course, an intellectual in any sense of the word") and by commitment ("by volunteering for and organizing a long dreary imaginary war in which America and the Present are fighting against Europe and the Past"); and that a comparison of *Paterson* with the *Four Quartets* clearly demonstrated Williams' defeat in "his long one-sided war with Eliot. . . ."[40]

Williams never wholly recovered from this criticism. He remembered it when speaking to Edith Heal of his *Selected Poems,* which had been published in 1949 with an introduction by Jarrell; and he retaliated unkindly by saying that Jarrell was "a clever man . . . still in his formative stages [and] likely to shift at any time."[41] That he still remembered — and was peevish — is a sign of his own continuing uncertainty about the achievement of the poem. In one sense, it may be said of *Paterson,* which has considerably more to recommend it than Jarrell realized, that it represents Williams' largest formal grasp of his culture and the very artwork (invention) that enabled him, at least, to transcend its logic of failure. The poet who made this poem has not failed in the way the poet in the poem has: Williams has been able to take up the materials of his particular place and make a poem of them, and he must be granted some recognition as a poet of his culture. In addition, he succeeds in showing the things for which he stood in his own time. The poem exhibits his urgent concern for invention and rehearses the old and always troublesome problem of a poet of culture: how, in behalf of invention, to make contact, to accept the materials of an environment for which he feels revulsion.

This tension is permanent in Williams' work and always appears when he is called on to respond as a poet of culture, or social-healer; and its dramatization in *Paterson* shows how greatly tasked he felt by the difficulties of the poem and by contemporaneous discussions of the situation of the poet. To have returned to what was always for him the initial decision and liberating act of poetry is understandable, yet now it represents renunciation, not of poetry but of the public function he had accepted in "The Wanderer." (*Paterson* is in many ways an extended, later "version" of "The Wanderer"; and Williams seems to have recognized this, when, in Book V, the book of memory uniting his beginning and his end, he incorporates in a new context significant lines from his first long poem.)[42] The poet in *Paterson* fails to fulfill the prophetic role demanded of him in "The Wanderer"— and Williams' misgivings about this role and the weariness that accompanied his effort to play it out in the writing of the poem are shown by the reluctance of the poet in the poem to be reconciled with his world.[43] (And why should he or Williams be reconciled to a waste land?

> Doctor, do you believe in
> "the people," the Democracy? Do
> you still believe — in this
> swill-hole of corrupt cities?
> Do you, Doctor?   Now?
>
> Give up
> the poem. Give up the shilly-
> shally of art.[44]

And how can he be reconciled when so strongly denied recognition by "criticism"?)

The failure of the poet in the poem expresses Williams' rejection of the very thing the poem makes good: his public career as a poet of culture. From this time forward — and chiefly by means of the transition provided by "The Desert Music"— he turned from the cultural to the personal aspects of his myth of America. The poet's discovery of America and his erotic exploration of it in search of Beautiful Thing —

> The thought returns: Why have I not
> but for imagined beauty where there is none
> or none available, long since
> put myself deliberately in the way of death?[45]

— this is replaced by a personal journey to love, the longest journey, that brought him home to his wife Flossie, who years before, at the beginning, had kindled that myth.[46]

:: four

The Autobiography originated in this crisis of achievement and reputation. Though written quickly — from December, 1950, to March, 1951 — it had been in preparation for some time. The autobiographical notes published in *Poetry* supplied more than the "first twenty or thirty pages" Williams mentioned in acknowledgment; they supplied the scenario for all of Part I and the first chapter of Part II, almost one-third of the book. Then Williams had been reminded of much that filled Part II when, in 1949, he turned up, in answer to a request by McAlmon for some old publications, "an astonishing lot of old stuff." Included were such things as Emanuel Carnevali's *A Hurried Man,* which otherwise would probably not have found a place in *The Autobiography,* and the diary of the trip to Europe in 1924, which provided important material that contributed to the shape of the book.[1] Part III, the concluding portion, was essentially an account of the celebrity he had recently achieved, and it may have been prompted by such things as the inclusion of his poems in Selden Rodman's *100 Modern Poems* (1949), where he figures twice, in a section on "Forerunners" and in the final section on "The 'Forties," and is also saluted in a poem by Kenneth Rexroth, "A Letter to William Carlos Williams."[2]

Correspondence, early in 1950, with Henry Wells over matters of family history and his career as a poet, and with the young Indian poet Srinivas Rayaprol over the difficulties of being a poet, clarified some basic themes. The facts of his origins and the wanderings of his French and English ancestors were set down correctly — and that he remembered his Grandmother Wellcome's repudiation by the Godwins of London which had been "the origin of her wanderings" suggests the tenuous yet profound associations of awakening memory. (The tutelary spirit of "The Wanderer" was this Cockney grandmother who had raised him. "I identified my grandmother with my poetic unconscious," Williams explained to John Thirlwall in 1956, "she was the personification of poetry" — so that their relations in the poem enact the breeding with himself in which his poetry began. She is also the environment, the "supplying female," the presiding deity of place. When the river of *Paterson,* which is also the river of "The Wanderer," returns to its beginnings in Book V, published in 1958, Williams is aware of his origins and consciously concludes with childhood memories already recorded in *The Autobiography,* climactic lines from "The Wanderer," and recollections of his grandmother's undoing and last words.)[3] To Wells he also complained of an oversight common in the criticism of his work, the failure "to take into consideration my role as a theorist." And then in explaining the social function of *Paterson* —"the poem to me (until I go broke) is an attempt, an experiment, a failing experiment, toward assertion with broken means but an assertion, always, of a new and total culture, the lifting of an environment to expression" — he found the ruling metaphor of the book: the poem as "the great (often final) blossom of a triumphant culture."[4]

He suggested later to his editor David McDowell that the title of *The Autobiography* should be "ROOT, BRANCH & FLOWER"; and it should have been because the organic metaphor accurately conveys his conception of art and life, and his own life, as he describes it, grew in that fashion and, remarkably, like the chicory lifting its flowers on bitter stems out of the scorched ground, had a splendid flowering.[5] Conrad Aiken, in the most perceptive review of *The Autobiography*, recognized this: "he has come to a late flowering and eminence, and an influence, too, that must be a source of great satisfaction to him, and the more so as it is deserved."[6] Yes, he had been satisfied and had managed to express it, but he had never been as certain as Aiken was of his desert. He had told Rayaprol of his jealousy of Dylan Thomas, whose successful readings seemed always to have preceded his own, and Wells of the "small hell" his "belated recognition" had brought him.[7]

The heart attack in 1948 had been a summons to autobiography. But Williams, even though he confessed at the time his doubts of living as long as his mother and grandmother, had not yet completed *Paterson* and was unwilling to be conclusive. He called his autobiographical installments "Some Notes Towards. . . ." and, with returning health, terminated them. Subsequent events, however, renewed the need for autobiography: the death of his mother, another stroke in 1949, and "the disheartening Library of Congress affair" which, according to Flossie, drove him into "a serious mental depression" and "set him back tragically. . . ." The Congressional response to his appointment to "the Chair of Poetry at the Library of Congress" was a blow whose force is indicated by Williams' silence in *The Autobiography* and difficulty, later, in speaking about it.[8] In "The F.B.I. and Ezra Pound," a chapter of *The Autobiography,* he tried, without relating the incident, to explain it and establish his unimpeachable loyalty; and even more distressing than the report of his protestations ("'Of course I'm a loyal American citizen. I-I-I've spent my whole life . . . for my country. . . .'") is the rollcall of the artists of his generation with which, for undisclosed emotional reasons, he concludes. This rollcall of frustrated, prostituted, abandoned careers, and mostly deaths is given in the present tense ("So here is Pound confined to a hospital for the insane in Washington; Bob McAlmon working for his brothers in El Paso; Hemingway a popular novelist; Joyce dead; Gertrude Stein dead. . . .") and offers a glimpse of the dreadful landscape of failure from which the writing of *The Autobiography* rescued him.[9] To write now, even if it were a conclusive act, was necessary in order to surmount emotional chaos; and Williams spoke truly when he told Edith Heal that for him writing this book had been "good therapy."[10]

But it had been good therapy only in the sense that, wanting "poetic justice," as Aiken recognized, he had secured it for himself.[11] *The Autobiography* is essentially a defense of the poet of culture, a disingenuous essay in vindication. Its art is apparent in the opening paragraph, where Williams, accepting the typical criticism of himself in an anecdote that he tells at his own expense, establishes a major theme, posture, and voice: "I was an innocent sort of child and have remained so to this day. Only yesterday, reading Chapman's *The Iliad of Homer,* did I realize for the first time that the derivation of the adjective venereal is from Venus! And I a physician practicing medicine for the past forty years. I was stunned!" Now innocence is something of which he is proud. Commenting on his first book, the privately printed *Poems* (1909), he said that "the first poem is called 'Innocense'. . . . I appear to be stating my case right from the beginning. The first line . . . reads, 'Innocense can never perish.' I really believed that then, and I really believe it now. It is something intrinsic in a man."[12] By beginning in this way, Williams characterizes both his past and present, and unites them. Innocence has given him the power and protection, the readiness and capability of living the American life he is going to describe. It is comparable to the "ignorance" that Wallace Stevens believed to be "one of the sources of poetry"; and Williams, who usually describes Shakespeare as "ignorant," claims it for himself when he identifies with Shakespeare as the mediator between the academy ("the Eliots") and the undisciplined but vital "dirt men" (Kenneth Patchen, for example).[13]

Innocence, of course, shades into naïveté, as in his failure to know the etymology of "venereal," but such naïveté is a come-on, as much a pose as Franklin's. In this way Williams *uses* his public image — the "Fresh-hearted daisy boy sitting/self-sunlit/on the wistful weather-beaten/front porch of America" of Robert Carlton Brown's poem.[14] Similarly, innocence shades into ignorance, not Stevens' variety but Pound's. The simple American is also what Pound unremittingly taunted Williams with being, the uneducated or undereducated American. And Williams suffered from that taunt because he took it seriously not in the person of Pound, whose ways he knew well from young manhood, but in the person of Eliot.[15] Eliot had always written him down as one of those "poets who have had little scholarship," and Williams, as he told Walter Sutton in one of his last interviews, "was intensely jealous of this man, who was so much more cultured than I was. . . ."[16]

The anxiety of ignorance — of lack of "Culture," of "reading," not lack of individual talent but lack of tradition — persisted for reasons so deep that even his learning in painting and medicine (especially well assimilated in his work) did not eradicate it.[17] This anxiety is the subject of poems like "The Controversy" and "Aigeltinger," the latter about a boyhood schoolmate whose achievement had shadowed him. In this poem the issue is expressed in the terms in which he considers it in *The Autobiography:* "They say I'm not profound," a criticism by scholars to which he replies by saying in reference to *Paterson,* that "the poet thinks with his poem, in that lies his thought, and that in itself is the profundity."[18] This appeal to the poem — to his inventiveness — answers another charge associated with ignorance: that he is a primitive. The recollection, at the beginning of *The Autobiography,* of the infant poet beating a drum in perfect time appears to support this, but actually it is intended to testify to his perfect ear and to prepare for his claim, carefully advanced in passages on poetic theory, of having discovered formal means appropriate to American experience, a fitting "measure."[19]

Innocence is both reality and pose in Williams, becoming the latter when he consciously uses the former. The innocence that is intrinsic and to which *The Autobiography* gives the impression that he has been true is of the kind conveyed by Charles Sheeler's photograph of the poet in his early forties: an intense expectation of wonder, and openness to self-renewal in the joy of perception. And what is remarkable is that the pose of innocence is a means by which this impression is created. There is, for example, the "ignorant" man who reads Homer — and Williams did at this time — but the *Iliad* and *Odyssey* are also important allusively. They are poems to be compared with *Paterson,* a "classic" example of the evocation of the "presence" of our culture; they are fables of the poet's adventure incorporated in *Paterson* ("Ulysses went out and returned intact").[20] Then the incredible confession that he had never seen the connection between venereal disease and Venus, when he was familiar with the one as a physician and with the other as a poet (Stevens might have been thinking of Williams when he wrote: "A poet looks at the world as a man looks at a woman").[21] The force of Williams' confession comes partially from his admission in the foreword that "I am extremely sexual in my desires" and that a man's secret lies "in the manner in which he directs that power. . . ."[22] His incredible innocence directs one's attention elsewhere: to the pursuit of Beautiful Thing, which has fully engaged him, and to his repudiation, in Part II of *The Autobiography,* of the Parisian life which depicts the darker, chaotic, abandoned side of himself that he denied. He does not wish to "possess" a woman but the Beautiful Thing of his own imagination — what Myra in *A Dream of Love* accurately describes as "the rape of the imagination," that pursuit of the self by the self finally realized in the later poems and in the hunt of the unicorn of *Paterson V.*[23]

Williams explains in *A Dream of Love* that, to protect his integrity, a "man must create a woman of some sort out of his imagination to prove himself. Oh, it doesn't have to be a woman, but she's the generic type." From the fact that he produces her "in full beauty out of the shell of his imagination," it is evident that Venus is her generic name; and when he possesses her in *A Dream of Love* he finds the death that in *The Autobiography* he sees in the "various perfections" of women.[24] His innocence, in this sense, may be very American; his quest of beauty is romantic. In the preface of *Paterson* he states: " 'Rigor of beauty is the quest. But how will you find beauty when it is locked in the mind past all remonstrance?' " *A Dream of Love*, the play closest to Williams' secret, is about this difficult quest; and *Paterson III*, which tells of the poet's encounter with Beautiful Thing, and *Paterson IV* (i), a drama in the manner and about the theme of *Many Loves*, are also especially concerned with it. At the end of *Paterson IV* the old poet has forgotten his "virgin purpose";[25] but the writer of *The Autobiography* has not forgotten because the quest is so much a part of his "innocence." This is the innocence upon which the doctor of *A Dream of Love* insists — and pleads for the understanding of his wife. For this "innocence" began in the poet's loss of innocence, in the erotic initiation of marriage; the doctor of *A Dream of Love* (and Williams in "Asphodel, That Greeny Flower") acknowledges this: "I died in everything. . . . From which you once rescued me — hence my devotion." He had discovered the ideal in the physical and had rigorously — too rigorously for his wife — followed after it.[26]

As an account of his innocence, *The Autobiography* bears this out by omitting all personal reference to Flossie after the brief story of courtship and marriage; by making marriage a decisive moment, the point of departure into the world of art; and by leading one to believe that Flossie willingly accepted it. Yet this quest is eventually renounced — with the completion of *Paterson IV* — and the old poet, who does connect venereal with Venus, goes back to the physical (for "warmth" and "comfort") in the sexual reverie of *Paterson V*, which develops the theme touched on in the pages on the "lost girls" of Paris in *The Autobiography*, and proclaims the morals of the whorehouse. In this respect, *The Autobiography* is a stage in the journey back to love and prepares for the fuller story of his courtship and marriage in *The Build-Up* (1952) and for the admission in "Asphodel, That Greeny Flower" that the light awakened at their marriage has not gone out but, like an odor,

> has revived for me
> and begun again to penetrate
> into all crevices
> of my world.[27]

Williams' use of innocence is cunning. Because of it we are quickly admitted to intimacy and he can humbly tell the story of the poet-doctor who was never, or not for long, at the center of the literary life. There is nothing "literary" in the presentation. The narrative is the work of the raconteur we know from the several collections of stories (two new stories are included in *The Autobiography*, "Our Fishman," on the fulfilled life, and "A Maternity Case," on birth; and there are anecdotes about a railroad porter, a babysitter's fake robbery, and a trip on Christmas day to the zoo). His warm and easy voice — some would say folksy, "vernacular" — determines the mode of narration; and the voice itself was chosen as a proper American medium. ("Am reading Faulkner's *Light in August* as I go along with my biography. It's a good American language traveling companion. That's important.")[28] Aiken speaks of the "calculated homespunness and naturalness, the conversational style" which fits this "somewhat rambling and disproportioned, book" — the style and method of the stories in which "the answers come slowly and confusedly" because the narrator is actually working through his materials.[29]

An artful artlessness reminds one of Franklin, who

used his autobiography to present an exemplary story of success. This, too, is Williams' purpose: to show, in the story of his success as a poet, how others might live (must live) the literary life in America. *The Autobiography* is written particularly for American aspirants. It presents a folk character fit to be placed in Constance Rourke's *American Humor:* the "country doctor" who comes to the city and to Europe (to Culture), who is out of it, marginal, uncelebrated, but succeeds at the end and has the last laugh — by writing his autobiography. (In the section on Paris, Williams recalls that "I was a rustic in my own eyes" and that Eliot appeared at the Dôme "in top hat, cutaway, and striped trousers.")[30] And this story of an *American* poet who has tried to further the work of Whitman is a "song of myself," which offers affirmative proof that the American environment is sufficiently consenting to nurture a poet — that one need not go to an alien culture for sustenance. Amid all the vicissitudes of experience (he conveys the sense of this by proceeding in a somewhat random, often abrupt fashion) he seems to pursue his art unwaveringly and to survive as a poet. His American nativity is fortunate, bringing him close to the primary culture of his locale — the "place" that diminishes the distance between past and present, that joins Kipp's Woods of his boyhood and the Paterson whose sights he now points out to his grandson, because he has *lived* in it and imaginatively mastered it. Without didactic insistence the book reveals the value of place to selfhood, success, survival; this is one of the ideas this book is an *autobiography of.* And for this reason (and others) one associates it with Frank Lloyd Wright's *Autobiography,* which turns so much about Taliesin, and the "American" childhood of Louis Sullivan's *Autobiography of an Idea,* both narratives of the nurture of

American genius. In this connection one thinks also of Thoreau because he not only traveled much in Concord[31] but in his essay on wild apples wrote the fable of American genius. All of these writers show that even though the American soil is often stubborn and the environment unfavoring, the growth of (firmly planted) genius is intrinsic, a flowering of the persistent self.

For Williams the representative artist in this respect is Edgar Allan Poe, who first asserted an "expression of a re-awakened genius of *place*" and was not slavish (no more than Williams) "BECAUSE he had the sense within him of a locality of his own, capable of cultivation."[32] This unusual view of Poe may be explained by Williams' identification — as also in the story of "Old Doc Rivers" — with a man whose refinement of sensibility is punished by a crude environment: "Poe could not have written a word without the violence of explosive emotion combined with the in-driving force of a crudely repressive environment. Between the two his imagination was forced into being. . . ." Poe was the first, not the last, "desert flower"; Whitman was forced "to come from under . . . through a dead layer."[33] And so had Williams and his New Jersey neighbor John Marin, both of them "growing from a split stem [of a weed!] in a certain patch of ground. . . ."[34]

The essential nurture, the root of American genius, it seems, is all in one's childhood. The doctors in *White Mule* and *In the Money* express such views of the formative significance of childhood, and these, in some ways, are exemplified in *The Autobiography*. The child is endowed with resistant individuality and from its first breath confronts the world, a particular world relations with which create its particular self. It is born into *a* world, is a "small prisoner . . . forced into the accidental mould of the life of [its] . . . parents"; every detail of life that encloses it leaves an imprint, and closed in, it seeks release, turns outward to the exciting prospect of "learning the world. . . ." These ideas are brilliantly presented in the fictive chronicle of the birth and growth of Flossie, and they are a clue to what is told and omitted in *The Autobiography,* where Williams does not construct a world for himself but presents himself living in a world already there, a world to be worked through to the realizations of self and art.[35]

The "First Memories" with which *The Autobiography* begins seem either trivial or inconsequential but of course are not, certainly not the memory of terror ("the terror that flared from hidden places and all 'heaven' ' ") which he says dominated his youth — a memory absent in the *Poetry* version and set down later in conjunction with his "first definable memory," that of being put out of doors "after the blizzard of '88. . . ." Both memories emerge from his present fear, the fear described and accepted in one of the wonderful last poems, "The Dance," where life is "this flurry of the storm/that holds us,/plays with us and discards us. . . ."[36]

The account of these formative years is scant, merely notation that, like the memory of terror, requires filling out. For example, almost all that really counts — still counts — in his relation with his father is only hinted at in the confession of the awful dream in which his father, returned to life, tells him his poems are bad. And put on record is the unusual household where French and Spanish were spoken and his mother held seances, yet the impression of its oddity is momentary. Notation answers Williams' demand for truthfulness but discloses little, and it permits him to create — such is his art — the vivid impression that his boyhood was typically American, that home mattered less than in fact it did, that the world he was learning was the "personal wild world" of the free, old time horse-culture. The boy who roamed Kipp's Woods ("our wilderness") with his BB gun and searched for flowers is a throwback to Natty Bumppo and the voluptuary Daniel Boone, the youth determined to be perfect, another Franklin. In his wild abandon as a boy and his resistance to authority in young manhood (see "Hell's Kitchen") he manifests the qualities he felt were characteristic of the American spirit. Very little is related of what in his environment repressed him ("I was a mighty unhappy pup," Doc says in *A Dream of Love*); the portrait of the artist as a boy is a happy one.[37]

When Conrad Aiken praised Williams' description of childhood, he probably had in mind an impression created not entirely by the abbreviated account of Part I but by the superimposition of nostalgic memories which introduce Part III.[38] In "A Look Back," Williams finally describes the rural village of his boyhood — and the present sense of these memories is powerful. He does this, as he had also in *Paterson IV*, because he wishes to measure change; and the sense of change is especially intense because in the previous chapter, ending Part II, he tells of a trip he had taken in 1931 in the hope of quitting urban life. On a voyage to Newfoundland, he found himself (as Thoreau had in Canada) facing the wilderness: "There . . . it was, stretching away . . . to the North Pole if I wanted to follow." And at the northernmost point of his travels he had taken, alone, a ritual dip in the Arctic Sea.[39] This episode is as skillfully placed as the episode ending Part I — that of his youthful travels in Spain where he "especially wanted to see Palos or Huelva, rather, from which Columbus had set sail on his first trip to America. . . ." It recalls the journey to the Maine Woods that had reminded Thoreau of "how exceedingly new this country still is"; and it suggests the further meaning, realized in the conclusion of *Paterson IV* (the swimmer emerging from the sea and going inland), of Thoreau's subsequent comment: "While the Republic has already acquired a history world-wide, America is still unsettled and unexplored."[40]

The theme of exploration is introduced in this fashion. It is a prominent theme of Williams, corresponding to his conception of the poet: "The poet should be forever at the ship's prow."[41] Subtly, it works with the dominant metaphor of growth, of root, branch, and flower; for the struggle of growth is not unlike the trials of Columbus. The American nativity of Part I is his root: "form'd from this soil, this air," said Whitman in "Song of Myself." The resurgence of art in America in the years before and after World War I with which he closely identified himself is his branch, the material of Part II. And his flower(ing), told in Part III, is the issue of steadfast allegiance, the poem *Paterson,* his furthest exploration (invention) in art of America, and his public acceptance as a poet.

At the end of Part I, covering the years 1883-1910, the young poet is on his "way back to the New World, with which [Williams says] my mind was teeming in those days." In Part II, "burning with the lust to write," he gives himself wholly to the cause of American art. During these exciting and turbulent years he was frequently in New York City (as doctor and as poet) and was much involved in the affairs of the new art — with painters and writers, the little theatre and the little magazines, especially with *Others* and his own *Contact,* intimate activities and daring enterprises that contributed to his style and aspiration as a literary man. "There was heat in us," he remembers, "a core and a drive that was gathering headway upon the rediscovery of a primary impetus, the elementary principle of all art, in the local conditions." But this resurgence of American art was halted by "the blast of Eliot's genius," by *The Waste Land,* whose appearance in 1922 was "the great catastrophe to our letters. . . ."

Except for the achievement of *Paterson,* which rises from the ruins of this disaster, the publication of *The Waste Land* is the occasion of greatest artistic moment in *The Autobiography.* Williams' story of its appearance "out of the blue," like an atom bomb, is not the less true as literary history for being melodramatic.[42] Eliot had in fact "turned his back on the possibility of reviving my world"; but whether he had so conclusively set Williams back twenty years or in certain ways so completely defeated him is not the impression of his own career given by the work he actually did or for that matter by *The Autobiography.* In speaking of the important function of little magazines in the battle for new art, Williams memorializes those talented men who did not survive: John Herrmann, Edward Lanham, Emanuel Carnevali, Paul Rosenfeld — some directly dependent on Robert McAlmon's help, all dependent on the intelligent support that men like McAlmon provide ("When a man like McAlmon goes down, others go with him").[43] But Williams himself survived.

The major event in the history of these years is the trip to Europe in 1924, which is less the test of allegiance it was in *A Voyage to Pagany* and *In the American Grain* (see "Père Sebastian Rasles") than a triumphal tour. The account fuses the actual present of the writer and the present of the travel diary (which is past) with the residue of the imagination that had shaped these materials in *A Voyage to Pagany*. Williams comments on the *"curious complications"* of this exercise in memory, but not for this reason did he omit his experiences in Italy and Austria. He was concerned almost entirely with Paris, with the great literary world and his fortunes in it; concerned to show that he had the talent and the reputation, that he had the option but chose otherwise.[44] "The sections on Paris, in that great make-heyday," Aiken says, "are an admirable extension of Cowley's notes on the subject."[45] Williams dwells on them because they record a watershed moment of his career and are the reference point for gauging the triumphs of Part III. But as he had found before the war, during a "fabulous week" in London, another literary center, the intense and thrilling atmosphere of the art world could be "fatiguing in the extreme": "I don't know how Ezra stood it," he says of the earlier experience, "it would have killed me in a month. It seemed completely foreign to anything I desired. I was glad to get away."

Carefully placed in Part II, as part of his explorations, are the first installments of his theory of art, which represent also a weapon — directives, manifestoes — in the battle for new art that he had used in the past and, in the recounting, was using still.[46] These theoretical statements unite past and present and provide one of the continuities of his career.[47] They have a progressive development and, while making *The Autobiography* a compendium of aesthetic theory, bind it together. Williams presents himself as theoretician as well as poet. In *Paterson IV* he shows the transmission of his poetic legacy by introducing Allen Ginsberg's letters; here he transmits the enabling theory, the chart to poetic discovery, and also introduces, as a recent addition to it, Charles Olson's pronouncements on projective verse.

Part III, which interested Williams more than the other parts, has a quality of the present that the others do not have.[48] It alone has an epigraph —

> "Old though I am, for lady's love unfit,
> the power of the beauty I remember yet."

These lines of Dryden's (inaccurately quoted) call up the life-long quest of Beautiful Thing ("the beauty"— Williams added the article) and announce the transformation by memory that will renew it as a personal journey to love. In the space of a few pages on the changes that have altered his boyhood world, he is able to create the sense of an entire life and to move easily into general considerations of the most important, the enduring elements of his life, and in this way he rededicates himself to them and expresses the creative necessity to go on that *The Autobiography,* formally, closes off.

There is, for example, the chapter "Of Medicine and Poetry," which has an unusual intensity because in it Williams is revealing his secret. Here he tells of his search for Beautiful Thing ("The thing, the thing, of which I am in chase. . . . To this day I am in pursuit of it"); of the "perfections" that he was aware of in the people about him (he had hardly used that notion since *Kora in Hell*); and of the "presence" he wished to capture (another notion prominent in early work, especially *A Voyage to Pagany*). He insists that in the course of his life he has seen the Beautiful Thing that has possessed him ever since a girl in the fifth grade (Nettie Vogelman in *The Great American Novel*) awakened his desire to pursue it.[49] And then, in an instance of the immediate past, he offers confirmation: "As Bob McAlmon said after the well-dressed Spanish woman passed us in Juárez (I had said, Wow! there's perfume for you!): 'You mean that?' he said. 'That's not perfume, I just call that whores.' "[50]

In the following chapter "The City of the Hospital" the themes of medicine and Beautiful Thing (the nurses are "the most beautiful women in the world") are resumed in a context, however, that deliberately repudiates Eliot's belief that "The whole earth is our hospital . . ." ("East Coker IV," *Four Quartets*). "The city of the hospital," Williams declares, "is my final home." And he adds: "Obviously, enough, the entire world today is a hospital so that, one thing canceling the other, that makes the hospital a very normal environment." Here, too, as in the previous chapter, cure is not as important as the chase: "Discovery is the great goal. . . ." That, and to learn thoroughly the nature of man, to be one of the "humane priests of healing," and to stand "in the front line, in the trenches."

Such is his world and his work, and the implication is that, sustained by it, he has been able to advance his conception of the poem and, at last, to overcome his rivals. Throughout *The Autobiography*, Pound is the poet against whom Williams sets himself and builds the picture of his achievement. He does not stand up to Pound directly or boast his success. In the chapter on projective verse, for example, he explains the theory in terms of the marriage of Charles and Musya Sheeler, marriage, like the poem, being a "construction." He praises Charles' vital way of using the past and Musya's ability "to transfer herself to the environment" and contribute to the new construction.[51] For he has seen, he says, "men and women run off from the pressing necessity of making a new construction"; and he knows, as he says in the concluding remark before turning to Pound, that "nothing can grow unless it taps into the soil."

The final chapter on Pound, placed between accounts of Williams' friendships, lecture tours, and rising reputation, is depressing. Williams visits his friend at St. Elizabeth's, and the careful, factual description of Pound's situation and behavior expresses his shock. He notes Pound's twitching hands and rushing, structure-less speech (see also *Paterson III*), and he sees in his face a likeness to "the beast of Cocteau's well-known film. . . ."[52] Pound seems unmoved by his confinement — and unmoved in his opinions ("His mind has not budged a hair's breadth"). But Williams is even more distressed by the gray old hospital with its barred win-dows, and by something he observes there — "this man, naked, full-on and immobile, his arms up as though climbing a wall, plastered against one of the high win-dows . . . like a great sea slug against the inside of a glass aquarium. . . ." This is for him the image of his horror at being in such a place, separated from the out-side world. His judgment of Pound, given by a taxi driver, is mild: " 'He ain't crazy,' he said. 'He just talk too much.' "

For himself these were not, in spite of illness, years of confinement, but of freedom and renewed contact. Something (sadly reminiscent) of the literary life of the 1920's was recaptured at writers' conferences, at Yaddo, and on the university lecture platform, and his explora-tion seems to have been fulfilled by the trips West that permitted him to see the country and extend his influence — to become truly national. The concluding, climactic portion of the book, about his last trip West in 1950, is full of the excitement of discovery, mission, and accep-tance. Williams has become an American hero of the sort he had celebrated in *In the American Grain*.[53]

Williams treats his lecturing with levity because, after all he had said against universities, he finds his

presence there anomalous. But what he says is serious
and adds heavily to the critical argument of the book.
He propounds a sexual theory of art based on the unhappy dualism of things ("everything we do is an effort
to achieve conjunction, not to say unity"); this glosses
the situation of Cress in *Paterson* ("women are neglected
in the arts"). He advances a theory of culture in which
art offers release from frustration ("allows us to beat our
enemy, the husband"), a theory, as the reference to "the
chief and all his women" indicates, that is also applicable to *Paterson*. Then he speaks of construction, an
essential distinction of modern art, as an example of the
inventive powers of man, and tellingly sets this discussion
against the carnage of western lumbering, evidence of the
continuing spoliation of the continent. Finally he reaches
the theme that matters most to him: the fate of poetry
in a society, even that of the West which faces the Orient,
that clings still to "worn-out Europe" and refuses the
adventure of the "new."

Williams' westward exploration tested the hopes of
a lifetime and probably awakened the sad realization
later expressed in "Asphodel, That Greeny Flower":

> ... take that other voyage
> which promised so much
>   but due to the world's avarice
>   breeding hatred
> through fear,
>   ended so disastrously;
>   a voyage
> with which I myself am so deeply concerned,
>   that of the *Pinta,*
>   the *Niña,*
> and the *Santa María.*
>   How the world opened its eyes!

```
                    It was a flower
            upon which April
                    had descended from the skies!
                    How bitter
            a disappointment!
                    In all,
                            this led mainly
            to the deaths I have suffered.
                    For there had been kindled
                    more minds
            than that of the discoverers
                    and set dancing
                            to a measure,
            a new measure!
                    Soon lost.
```

Experience of the West revived his interpretation of the failure of American culture: "Here was I a visiting lecturer in English, with a 'new' theory of art to propound, looking at this decay, somewhat affected by its perverse logic. . . . What should be new is intent upon one thing, the metaphor — the metaphor is the poem. [But] There is for them only one metaphor: Europe — the past. All metaphor for them, inevitably so, is the past: that is the poem. . . . They don't live, they metaphorize."[54] Yet — such again is the precarious balance of failure and success, despair and hope — there were the students to whom he had spoken of this, in particular the students at Los Angeles who seemed to understand and whose ovation crowned his trip; and there were the old friends of other times and places who made the event a personal one of homecoming.

The last chapter on *Paterson,* which follows, is also a theoretical statement. It recapitulates what Williams had said already about the futility of "cures" and the supreme value in poetry of "presence"; and it justifies his life's work — "to find an image large enough to embody the whole knowable world about me." *Paterson* is such a construction, a new metaphor, not of Europe but of his own place. It is his conclusive example of the art of the local that is therefore universal ("it would be as itself, locally, and so like every other place in the world").

And fittingly, the story of his life ends in this place, with the poet guiding his grandson and a visitor over the intimate terrain, pointing out the sources of the river, the symbol uniting his life and the history of the region — the last spring at Great Notch, all the others filled up, diverted, fouled — and pointing out the place where Mrs. Cumming and Sam Patch leaped. Standing at the edge of the falls, he is not compelled to leap as they were because, unlike them, he has been articulate. This is the meaning and the measure of his success as a poet: in his art, speech had not failed him and he had shown, as he said of those whose presence and perfections had compelled his art, the daring of "the longest leap."[55] He had been able, accordingly, to be a poet of his culture, and to make his poem a seed, a bearer of new life in another time. In the perspective of *The Autobiography, Paterson* becomes what Williams hoped it would be, the flowering of his culture and the achievement of a lifetime — and the warrant of the statement, made when first considering Eliot, that only now were we beginning to recover from his impact.[56]

:: five

The Autobiography, so equable in tone, so full of the sense of fulfilled life, satisfied Williams' desire to clarify his purpose and justify himself. Like *Walden*, it appropriated for the writer what the writer himself, except in this particular way, had been unable to. As such, it was a victory of art.

But in another way, the victory of art was not so pleasing. Having given his life a determinate shape — having in art objectified himself — he had conferred upon himself the immortality of art at the expense of his own vital impulse.[1] This desire, originating in the apprehension of death, had been an initial motive of *The Autobiography*, and the stroke he had toward the end of writing it probably led him to conclude the book with a testamental action.

This aspect of the writing of the book betrayed its autobiographical nature — the fact that "true autobiography," as Roy Pascal says, "can be written only by men and women pledged to their innermost selves."[2] Williams gives the impression that he is pledged to a never-ending search for the secret gardens of the self, yet in fixing himself in art, he is untrue to the deepest truth of his self: its restlessness, its imperious need for release.[3] The act of composition, which he said early gave him the greatest excitement and of which he said late (in "Asphodel, That Greeny Flower") he regretted most the termination, may have deceived him with its living motion.[4] He seems to have realized this (as he says in "Asphodel, That Greeny Flower," "If a man die/it is because death/ has first/possessed his imagination") and that the only action that could overcome the "death" of *The Auto- biography* was that of poetry. To feel almost immedi- ately and so terribly, desperately, as he does in "The Desert Music," the need to affirm his vocation as poet ("I *am* a poet!") is to feel the need to affirm his contin- uing existence; it is a way of saying that he is alive, still ready to meet life and accept its "worry and unrest."[5]

And with this, he seems to have fully grasped from his preoccupation with memories the fact of memory that he declared in "The Descent": that it does not confine the self but opens for it a new field for discovery, a new realm of life, and in the evening time enables the poet to overcome despair.

> The descent
>   made up of despairs
>   and without accomplishment
>   realizes a new awakening:
>   which is a reversal
>   of despair.

This poem states his faith in the unconquerable self, in the irrepressible force of its life; and it prefaces the action of self-recovery in "The Desert Music," an action of the kind he had performed at the close of *Paterson II*.[6]

There, having almost yielded to his despair of being the poet he had set out to be and confronting again the "She" (both the "supplying female" and his own "poetic unconsciousness") who admonishes him, as he had been in "The Wanderer," to "Be reconciled, poet, with your world," he actually accomplishes the "reversal." He breaks down "the pinnacles of his moods" and from this base regains "the sun kissed summits of love!" The movement — "the descent follows the ascent" — is a representative act of the poet's mind, for reversal answers to the restlessness and need for release that characterize his rhythm of creation. And when the reversal occurs, there is a poem (within the larger poem) to show for it, a poem, echoing perhaps an autumnal cadence of Poe ("On this most voluptuous night of the year"), that celebrates a perfect, serene springtime anticipating love. With this poem, the poet accepts the conditions of poetry he had despaired of satisfying and pledges himself to the pursuit of Beautiful Thing ("her belly is like a white cloud"). By writing the poem, he proves himself.

The pleasures of *The Autobiography* do not seem to have outlasted its completion. The malaise of finishing it was transferred to "The Desert Music" by way of the incident, briefly noted in the penultimate chapter of *The Autobiography,* that provided its occasion:

Juarez, across the bridge. Three cents the trip. *Sur le pont d'Avignon* — is all I could think of. The sparrows at night in the park — Bob and his brothers, George and Alec and their wives — tequilla at five cents a glass, a quail dinner and the Mexicans, the poor Indians — one huddled into a lump against the ironwork of the bridge at night — safe perhaps from both sides, incredibly compressed in a shapeless obstruction — asleep.[7]

Much of the matter of the poem is given here and also a bar of the music that moves the poem more than the poem itself helps us realize: a music of memory — here the memory of the opening phrase of the eighteenth-century French folksong Williams undoubtedly had learned in his youth, either at home or in Europe.

One cannot trace all the nodes through which the force of this memory is transmitted. But clearly it is a memory of France and, in the context of this notation, of his visits there in the 1920's, especially the gala visit of 1924, which meant so much to him. In "The Desert Music" he says that en route to El Paso to meet Robert McAlmon he had slept "fitfully" — "Thinking of Paris, I waked to the tick/of the rails. . . ." McAlmon had been one of his associates in the literary cause Williams believed Eliot had defeated; together, at the beginning of the 1920's, they had edited *Contact*. And McAlmon, who soon left for Paris, had furthered Williams' career (and the cause) by publishing in his Contact Editions and at the Three Mountains Press of Bill Bird the early demonstrations, *Spring and All* and *The Great American Novel*. To think of Paris was to think of this good friend —"Paris was his very twin"— and of that time when he and Flossie had come to Europe and McAlmon was an important figure there, his sponsor in avant garde circles.[8]

The grand occasion of that visit had been the supper in Williams' honor at the Trianon, attended by many of those writers and artists we now celebrate, most notably Joyce. Williams' recollection of that evening, recorded fully in both *A Voyage to Pagany* and *The Autobiography*, is a proud one marred only by the vivid memory of the inappropriate speech he had made. In the version of this episode in *A Voyage to Pagany*, Evans [Williams] "said something stupid in his embarrassment . . . — something he never forgave himself for saying, and Jack [McAlmon] heard it." The event is similarly reported in *The Autobiography* and is not important for the speech itself ("I had observed that when a corpse, in its hearse, plain or ornate, was passing in the streets, the women stopped, bowed their heads and that men generally stood at attention with their hats in their hands") but for the hostility that had prompted it. This feeling, which in *A Voyage to Pagany* had made him feel "uneasy," is more openly admitted in *The Autobiography:* "What had I to say with all eyes, especially those of the Frenchmen, gimleted upon me to see what this American could possibly signify, if anything? I had nothing in common with them." Though Williams portrays himself, especially in *A Voyage to Pagany,* as uncaring, he obviously cared deeply about his reception; and his behavior, in its unconscious origins and irreverence so much like Mark Twain's at the Whittier birthday dinner, was something he always regretted.[9]

Uncertainty is the burden of this memory of Paris, and uncertainty may have awakened it on the occasion of the dinner, again in a foreign land, with McAlmon and his brothers and their wives, the dinner described in "The Desert Music" at which Williams was greeted with the uncomfortable challenge, "So this is William/Carlos Williams, the poet. . . ." The occasion of the dinner in Juárez was probably more distressing than the earlier one if only because time had not dispelled the uncertainty and everything about the occasion was on the diminished scale the years know how to produce. McAlmon, who was broken in health and working now for his brothers in El Paso, is listed in *The Autobiography* among those writers of Williams' generation who are "dead": McAlmon, with whom his literary relations had been closer even than with Pound, who had been in some ways a double who dared where he had not, or the son whose going off had grieved him ("I wish I had the boy back with me," he had written Amy Lowell in 1921, "and not lost there abroad, to no good purpose I feel sure. My God, have we not had enough Pounds and Eliots? *The Sacred Wood* is full of them and their air rifles. But perhaps Bob will do better").[10] The battlefield of a generation's achievement, which may be visited wherever one finds a contemporary, is seldom pleasant to survey; to greet a contemporary may underscore the doubts of achievement that had quickened already the need for autobiographical self-assessment and vindication. And one might prefer to dine alone than in the company of philistines for whose sake one has spent his life — well-meaning people who, closely observing, announce the normality of the poet and ask impossible questions about his art.

The situation of the poet in "The Desert Music" recalls the situation of the poet who, in *A Voyage to Pagany,* was seized in the darkness by "the terror of no form." For beneath the calm surface of incident, the poem reveals the poet's state of chaos, the state of disintegration in which Williams found himself after completing *The Autobiography.* One speaks of this state of break-up as disintegration because it is not that "happy time," similar to it, "when the image becomes broken or begins to break up, becomes a little fluid. . . ."[11] It is the phase of descent, not the phase of ascent. Still, it is a necessary condition of poetry and of what the act of poetry insures: self-making and renewal.[12] What makes the anguish of "The Desert Music" so intense is Williams' need to be assured of his role of poet when he had shown in *The Autobiography* that this vocation had been for much of his life the strongest strand of his identity. If he needed *The Autobiography* to give his life permanence, he needed poetry to redintegrate the self — to restore, in contact with the world, the very chaos from which the ordering movement of imagination saved him.[13] This is especially the case in "The Desert Music," where, in turning to memory, the chaos of things already known, he reconstructs the world it had taken him a lifetime to make and so reconstructs the self. The things of this poem are familiar, the realities of his previous poetic endeavor, and having them to live with in his mind, he can now, by descent, discover them within rather than without himself. The inwardness of his materials — the fact that they are bound in the time of the self — accounts for their symbolic character (unusual for a poet who in his early poems was so little symbolic), for the reverberations of meaning which, fittingly, are the music he hears as well as the new spaces memory opens. The poem is about this aspect of making poems, about working through the terror to the assurance that underwrites composition. By some wonderful agency hard to describe, a successful poem gets made in the process, but the poem itself is mostly about the "distresses [that] can happen in the effort . . . to release ourselves to the imagination. . . ." The poem, in which a music heralds that "happy time" when "rigidities yield," ends with its own beginning.[14]

The poem begins as abruptly as the movement of the imagination, which figures here, as it had for Williams ever since the early poems and the improvisations of *Kora in Hell,* as a dance:

— the dance begins: . . .

The dance of the imagination with the materials of the poem, the memory of the visit to El Paso, has begun; the poem, and the dance it enacts and by which it comes into being and acquires form, has begun. (". . . a poem is tough by no quality it borrows from a logical recital of events nor from the events themselves but solely from that attenuated power which draws perhaps many broken things into a dance giving them thus a full being.")[15] To say that the dance begins is also to invoke it by declaring it: to rouse the sleepy mind to the object projected here and so prominent in the memory of this episode, the object with which the poet, in the course of the poem and especially at the end, intently dances.

> — the dance begins: to end about a form
> propped motionless — on the bridge
> between Juárez and El Paso — unrecognizable
> in the semi-dark

These introductory lines are, as Williams says in the story "Danse Pseudomacabre," an "invitation to the dance": "Either dance or annihilation."[16] They may be connected, perhaps because of the conjunction of beginning and end, with the memory, which he found curious, of *Sur le pont d'Avignon,* for on that bridge, "L'on y danse, l'on y danse. . . . L'on y danse tout en rond." And they should stand separately as a statement of the present action of the imagination — the composition of the poem — and as a frame for the recollection — itself an act of imagination — of the excursion of the imagination in El Paso–Juárez that follows.

To dance, above all, is to enter into the motions of life. It is an action, a movement, a process. The dance of life is not so much a metaphor as a fact; to dance is to know oneself alive, and to celebrate it.[17] This intense desire for the motion of life — to move in consonance with its rhythms — is expressed in "Ballet," a poem published in 1916, which has the shape of the dance, of a pirouette.[18] In this poem an exhilarating descent is opposed to the finished, rigid, formal, abstract aspects of ascent; for ascent, here, is not represented as a phase in the organic process of growth but as a "higher" level of life associated with religion and idealism, and especially with puritanical striving. The poet rejects all effort that is aspiring, that produces the spiritual "malady of the ideal"; he rejects all forms of immobility — the archaic, the past, winter, night, death. He wants the robin labor-

ing in song in the winter trees to "come down," to join
him (be one of the band of "grotesque fellows" he calls
for in "Sub Terra") in the loosening-up and letting-go
that make the dance the harbinger and creator, the very
motion of spring. The dance that he imagines will bring
in the day and the spring creates life out of the dust, out
of death; it is a whirlwind:

> Here in the middle
> of the roadway
> we will fling
> ourselves round
> with dust lilies
> till we are bound in
> their twining stems!
> We will tear
> their flowers
> with arms flashing!

Such behavior will astonish (his neighbors), for nothing
is more astonishing than life; but having participated in
its advent — a folk hero, say, like Davy Crockett, setting
the world in motion — he can bear the daily round, the
"wheels and/the pounding feet" that "crush forth/our
laughter," a Nietzschean joy. For this poem about the
dance is also a dance, an act of creation; and as Wallace
Stevens says of poems, it "refreshes life. . . ."[19]

The refreshment of life is perhaps as good a definition as any of what the work of imagination accomplishes. This exceedingly complex kind of work involves
several kinds of dancing or action: that of coming into
contact with the world, that of discovering the particular
motions of particular things, and that of creating (inventing, composing) the poem, which is itself the result
of the previous actions in the world and an objective
representation of them on the plane of the imagination.

Williams, who was as much concerned as Stevens with this wonder-working agency, first treated these primary aspects of imagination in *Kora in Hell,* where meditation on them was a part of the radical reassessment he was making of the poetry of his time.[20] Contact, for example, was a problem because what he wished to contact, and to use as the stuff of poetry, was "vulgar" — the common ("non-poetic") stuff of the world about him that he hoped, by means of the imagination, to "lift . . . out of the ruck."[21] To find *Kora in Hell* describes not only the state of beautiful things in America but a necessary condition (descent) of the imagination that he believed bestowed beauty by raising things — by rescuing, repairing, completing them.[22] "Look down," he advised Alva Turner in 1920; "Mister Preacher, do not forget that you are a poet too."[23] To bring Eurydice back was the work he proposed for the imagination — in this sense every poem it fashioned was a beautiful thing. Later statements such as "Poetry can be used to dignify life, which is so crass and vulgar" and "I have always tried to lead an elevated life [he means that he wished to live on the plane of the imagination]" reduce to the banal a heroic conception and betray a residual gentility.[24] And this had always been part of the problem of contact: to overcome the "secret arrogance" of gentility that kept him from being "tuned to these measures," the music of things about him; to break through — hence the destructive energy of *Spring and All* — the barrier of art itself, which stood between him and "his consciousness of immediate contact with the world."[25] When he does so in *Kora in Hell,* he hears music "out of the ground" and dances with the natural things about him.[26]

The dance is Williams' fundamental image of the poetic process, the poem, and even the poem's reception.

For dancing is joining with: in the dance one knows no dualism, but in a wholly natural way enters into and becomes vitally a part of things.[27] Such romanticism precludes the visionary uses of the imagination; and however much Williams exalts it — the imagination is his principle of life, of being and becoming — he does not separate it from the "immediacy" of things, the "actuality of every day," the "music of events."[28] These, in fact, quicken it. The imagination thrives on contact, not on withdrawal, dream, or angelic flight; without contact the dance cannot begin.

These notions of the action of the imagination in the world are part of a major tendency of modern thought with which we are already familiar in the work of philosophers of environment like Dewey and in the work of psychologists like Frederick Perls, Ralph Hefferline, and Paul Goodman, who, in *Gestalt Therapy,* brilliantly explain what poems like Williams' do.[29] But we are not as familiar with poetry which demonstrates these notions — notions alien to our theories of poetry which, in turn, account for the difficulty critics have in describing Williams' work. He himself has been his own best commentator, calling attention to such matters (to cite chapter titles from the above manual) as "contacting the environment" and "techniques of awareness." In *Spring and All,* where the poems are demonstrations of the theoretical statements, he tells us, in what might be an exercise in awareness, that "so much depends" upon the red wheelbarrow — so much awareness, which is characterized "by *contact,* by *sensing,* by *excitement* and by *Gestalt* formation."[30] So much depends upon how one sees the red wheelbarrow, on the right way of seeing. This he humorously depicts in "The Right of Way":

In passing with my mind
on nothing in the world

but the right of way
I enjoy on the road by

virtue of the law —
I saw

an elderly man who
smiled and looked away

to the north past a house —
a woman in blue

who was laughing and
leaning forward to look up

into the man's half
averted face

and a boy of eight who was
looking at the middle of

the man's belly
at a watchchain —

The supreme importance
of this nameless spectacle

sped me by them
without a word —

Why bother where I went?
for I went spinning on the

four wheels of my car
along the wet road until

I saw a girl with one leg
over the rail of a balcony[31]

In this poem the "open road" provides the "right way"
of experiencing; for travel, as in Whitman and Thoreau,
is a mode of experience by which one may be "trans-

ported." The couplets fit the experience of motion and brief glimpses, and follow the serial, expectant nature of seeing things, which he finds faster than thought. "Where I went" suggests the movement of an object toward a place, but "I went spinning" suggests the important vital movement, or dance, and the state of wonder of the poet for whom the human "spectacle," so perceived, is endlessly exciting and necessary.

It is necessary because Williams' vision is unmediated. Both the eye and the world it sees are in motion, creating the dizzy chaos, the lack of focus, that terrifies him and that the imagination, in all of its powers, helps him to overcome. By means of the senses, the sympathetic agencies of the imagination, he contacts his environment — "belongs to his world and time, sensually, realistically"; and by means of perception, an imaginative act, he locates a particular object in the flux and dances with it — understands it "in its natural colors and shapes," discovers its "perfections," its inner order or rhythm, and feels it "moving within himself."[32] What he says about the necessity of identification to the dramatist is applicable here: identification with things allows him to steal "the form by feeling it." As he says in *Kora in Hell,* he does not want to see *"floating visions of unknown import but the imaginative qualities of the actual things being perceived accompany their gross vision in a slow dance, interpreting as they go."*[33]

Many of Williams' poems perform this slow dance of the eye with the thing and give "the truth of the object," the "intense vision of the facts" and the "simple clarity of apprehension" that he values so highly.[34] Even though it is not exactly a poem, one might cite as an example the following "improvisation," which he calls a dance: "This is a slight stiff dance to a waking baby whose arms have been lying curled back above his head upon the pillow, making a flower — the eyes closed. Dead to the world! Waking is a little hand brushing away dreams. Eyes open. Here's a new world."[35]

The controlling feature of the dance is measure, which is determined by the organic quality of the thing perceived and, in turn, determines the movement, and form, of the poem. Once one has put himself in the way of this experience of the world, the difficulty is in finding the measures of things. "The trick of the dance," Williams says, "is in following   now the words, *allegro,* now the contrary beat of the glossy leg. . . ."[36] But the exact measure is supremely important because it gives the intrinsic truth of the thing — is a truth of the natural world that the imagination, by building the poem carefully, transfers to the world of art, to an object separate from nature yet by means of this common property true to it. Poetry, which Williams believed "began with measure . . . with the dance," is therefore one of the necessary instruments by which we order our world (the world of which we are a part); and it is all the more valuable because the order it provides is vital — "is in its vigor the process of ordering — a function of the imagination. . . ."[37] There is never "a poetic form of force and timeliness," he says, "except that which is in the act of being created. . . ." When invention and composition are successful, the "intrinsic movement" of the poem verifies its authenticity.[38]

These considerations of what making poems means to Williams explain his trust in "the hierarchies of the imagination" and his insistence that "to measure is all we know. . . ."[39] He ends the last book of *Paterson* with this summary statement of the human condition:

                        We know nothing and can know nothing
                                    but
                        the dance, to dance to a measure
                        contrapuntally,
                                    Satyrically, the tragic foot.

The dance of life, which is all we can know, is of tragic
origin. *"Out of bitterness itself,"* he wrote in *Kora in
Hell,* *"the clear wine of the imagination will be pressed
and the dance prosper thereby."*[40] And toward the end
of his life he declared that "only the dance is sure!/make
it your own." In "The Dance," the poem from which
these lines are taken, he presents clearly the world of
enveloping snow in which to live in one's life, by imagination, is the only fulfillment.

                        When the snow falls the flakes
                        spin upon the long axis
                        that concerns them most intimately
                        two and two to make a dance

                        the mind dances with itself,
                        taking you by the hand,
                        your lover follows
                        there are always two,

                        yourself and the other,
                        the point of your shoe setting the pace,
                        if you break away and run
                        the dance is over

                        Breathlessly you will take
                        another partner
                        better or worse who will keep
                        at your side, at your stops

                        whirls and glides until he too
                        leaves off
                        on his way down as if
                        there were another direction

gayer, more carefree
spinning face to face but always down
with each other secure
only in each other's arms

But only the dance is sure!
make it your own.
Who can tell
what is to come of it?

in the woods of your
own nature whatever
twig interposes, and bare twigs
have an actuality of their own

this flurry of the storm
that holds us,
plays with us and discards us
dancing, dancing as may be credible.[41]

The opening lines of "The Desert Music" summon
the poet to the dance of life at the same time that they
acknowledge his awareness that the end, whether of art
or life, is "a form/propped motionless." He sees the end
in the act of beginning, and his awareness of death gives
the creative action of the poem its steady intensity and
perhaps, compensatorily, prompts him to make a form
that represents a beginning. When he exclaims, "Wait!"
it is therefore both an outcry of the present moment and
a detail of the past incident, which he goes on to relate.
Now, finding the shapeless shape on the bridge is not in
the chronological order of the actual experience, though
it is in the order of his creative experience and memory —
the way in which both orders of experience support each
other is one of the remarkable aspects of the poem. The
Indian asleep on the bridge is never as explicitly defined
in the poem as he is in *The Autobiography,* for in the
poem he is the very stuff of the poem upon which the

poet works the creative act: an "Egg-shaped" thing, the poet suddenly recognizes, which he fertilizes and gives life in the making of the poem. This is the common un-formed material that he finds on the right of way ("on the very walk itself"), pauses to look into ("inspects"), and begins to move about with his imagination; and it is also the "old, dark America" the discoverers confronted[42] and his own primal pagan ground. It is appropriately placed here because it represents his poetic practice and because he is presenting a descent, his characteristic way of going down and out. He had always found release in the life of the social class beneath his own, but something more attracts him here: his identification with the dere-lict and old, the shapeless and dead ("a very shriveled old man./Maybe dead"), and his need to undergo once more, by writing a poem, the terror of birth (the shape-less shape is embryonic: "knees hugged tight up into the belly") and the "agony of self-realization."

Contact is the first sally of creation and brings the awareness of potentiality in materials ("Egg-shaped!"). It starts the poet pondering the creative act — "How shall we get said what must be said?" — which is an interior thought of the past occasion as well as the poet's thought in the present action of the poem. "Only the poem," is his answer to this question.

> Only the counted poem, to an exact measure:
> to imitate, not to copy nature, not
> to copy nature
>
> NOT, prostrate, to copy nature
> but a dance! to dance
> two and two with him —
> sequestered there asleep
>
> . . . .
>
> Only the made poem, the verb calls it
> into being.

In the text, these and other lines of similar import express the urgency, and difficulty, of the poet's need to create, to get said what *must* be said and can only be said, as the context indicates, by going beyond "the law," the dead forms ("The law gives us nothing/but a corpse, wrapped in a dirty mantle") that impose a restrictive order.[43] In "The Basis of Faith in Art," where the question of order is at issue, Williams tells his brother that "I was early in life sick to my very pit with order that cuts off the crab's feelers to make it fit into the box." One of the things he appreciated in going down and out was the vital order, the order of disorder, in the lives of the poor. "Never an order discovered in its living character of today," he said in another essay of this time, "always an order imposed in the senseless image of yesterday — for a purpose of denial." When his brother characterizes the poet's mind as disorderly, he replies: "If to have a mind in which order is broken down to be redistributed, then you are right, not otherwise."[44]

The mind so described is the kind of mind that has been at work in modern art. It is the kind of mind that Williams had been explaining in his critical essays almost from the beginning of his advocacy of the cause of newness. In an early essay on Joyce, for example, he defines Joyce's style as "truth through the breakup of beautiful words"; and in commenting on the painting of Juan Gris, his most frequent example of what he himself was attempting to do, he points out an essential distinction of the modernist departure — that between copying and imitating nature. Copying is a crude process, hardly creative, a "plagiarism after nature" that produces illusion rather than realism. The illusion of reality is commonly confused with realism, but realism, in Williams' view, is actually "of the imagination," what the mind makes of the world, its formalistic appropriation and re-distribution of things on its own plane, as in a painting by Gris, where things familiar to us in our experience are detached "from ordinary experience to the imagination." ("Here is a shutter, a bunch of grapes, a sheet of music, a picture of sea and mountains [particularly fine] which the onlooker is not for a moment permitted to witness as an 'illusion'. One thing laps over on the other, the cloud laps over on the shutter, the bunch of grapes is part of the handle of the guitar, the mountain and sea are obviously not 'the mountain and sea', but a picture of the mountain and the sea. All drawn with admirable simplicity and excellent design — all a unity —")

This disposition of things after the order of the imagination is creation, an activity of man that imitates the creative working of nature (what Emerson called the "method of nature") at the same time as it transforms, adds to, and enlarges nature. Williams agrees with Stevens, that "In the world of words, the imagination is one of the forces of nature." As he explains again in *The Autobiography* — the explanation is introduced at the proper chronological point and represents the early discussion — "It is NOT to hold the mirror up to nature that the artist performs his work. It is to make, out of the imagination, something not at all a copy of nature, but something quite different, a new thing, unlike any thing else in nature, a thing advanced and apart from it."[45]

The lines on copying and imitating nature in "The Desert Music" are not meaningful in themselves and require this elucidation. They enter the poem as a "trace" of one of the poet's deepest concerns and help define for us the test that making this poem was for him. One can imagine in some form less explicit the occurrence of such thoughts on the occasion of making any poem; they occur explicitly here because he had recently formulated them in *The Autobiography* and, during the period in which he composed the poem, in a letter to Frank L. Moore. In this letter, where the consideration of art is connected with the attempt to remain fully conscious and serene in the face of death, Williams says: "To copy nature is a spineless activity; it gives us a sense of our mere existence but hardly more than that. But to imitate nature involves the verb: we then ourselves become nature, and so invent an object which is an extension of the process." In similar words but more precisely he says in *The Autobiography:* "To imitate nature involves the verb to do. To copy is merely to reflect something already there, inertly: Shakespeare's mirror is all that is needed for it. But by imitation we enlarge nature itself, we become nature or we discover in ourselves nature's active part. This is enticing to our minds, it enlarges the concept of art, dignifies it to a place not yet fully realized."[46]

On the verb "to do" he had commented (and playfully demonstrated its powers) in "To Have Done Nothing," the sixth poem in *Spring and All.*

> . . . to do
> is capable
> of an
> infinity of
> combinations

To do is what all verbs, as parts of speech expressing action, do. To do is to make, to make something (of anything) by combining with anything ("infinity of/ combinations"). To do is verbal action, the dance; and to do is the spermatic element of language that becomes articulate — articulates — by finding its object. At the end of "The Desert Music," "The verb detaches itself/

seeking to become articulate." The entire poem works toward this moment and, in an applicable phrase of *A Voyage to Pagany,* expresses the poet's "lust to make."[47]

For he must make, not "vomit it up" in order to "escape." Writing of Shakespeare and of how he escaped by means of the imagination, Williams says that "he speaks authoritatively through invention, through characters, through design." And in *Paterson V* (which incorporates almost all of "Tribute to the Painters") he says, in regard to the necessity of breaking up old forms, that "you cannot be/an artist/by mere ineptitude"; and he commends, as an example of the work of the imagination, "Pollock's blobs of paint squeezed out/with design!" Design is the requisite thing — the fact that "in their designs" men have learned to shatter "the tyranny of the image"— for design is not only composition but also measure and involves the dance by which one moves in and with the world, is

> bound into a whole
> by that which surrounds us[48]

That which surrounds us, we learn in the course of "The Desert Music," is not only the world in which we are and of which we are the center, but an enveloping music, the sound, at first "insensate," that awakens motion, the dance. The poet's desire to dance with the sleeping shape awakens the music that "supersedes his composure," the action referring to both the poet and the shape, to the fixity from which both begin to stir. For both — such are the uses of ambiguous expression — are old men who have been asleep, Rip Van Winkles awakened by a "hallooing to us/across a great distance." The shape is any part of the world of which the poet makes a poem, and by making it affirms himself; but it is also the poet himself, that part of him that had fallen asleep and must now be roused to its inescapable work, the "agony of self-realization" that is the making of the poem. "Be patient," Williams writes in "To Daphne and Virginia" —

> Be patient that I address you in a poem,
>> there is no other
>> fit medium.
> The mind
>> lives there. It is uncertain,
>> can trick us and leave us
> agonized. But for resources
>> what can equal it?[49]

Failing the poem by which the mind builds anew, he feels that he, as much as the "shriveled old man," should be carted away and dumped into the river:

> Heave it into the river.
> A good thing.

This comment is probably made by one of his companions on his walk. (How little they are aware of the thoughts of the poet, yet how much the thoughts he has and their resolution depends on them! This poem is unique in having for its personnel his most intimate companions, the friend who shared his early career, and Flossie, who now, for the first time, accompanies him on the journey of a poem.) The comment is the judgment he passes on himself toward the end of the poem: "So you're a poet?/a good thing to be got rid of —." The image is a powerful one because it recalls both the ritual immersion in the filthy Passaic of "The Wanderer" with which he began his career as an *American* poet and the consummation of discovery that had fascinated him in the case of De Soto. In his beginning is his end, to be cast into the river: "Here," he writes of De Soto in *The Great American Novel,* "he had confronted the New World in all its mighty significance and something had penetrated his soul so that in that hour of need he had turned to this Mighty River rather than do any other thing." To give himself to the river so that "Europe should pass . . . into a new world" would be a "good thing."[50] But the poet, who had just crossed the country and the desert, is not yet ready (he will be readier at the end of *Paterson V*) and thinks instead of survival, of his memories of Paris, and of the poetic work he must now do to fulfill the prophecy of the "She" in "The Wanderer," who in "Soothsay" had enabled the poet to "Behold yourself old!/Sustained in strength, wielding might in gript surges!" The need to survive had first compelled the music. ". . . the fertile desert,/(were it to get water)," he recalls having thought, "surrounded us, a music of survival, subdued, distant, half/heard." And so, turning now to the poetic work of imitating nature — "to place myself (in/my nature) beside nature"— he says, in words richly significant, "I lay myself down. . . ."

In a literal sense, Williams means that he will give a full account of what happened to him; and he begins by telling of the Old Market in Juárez, where he and Flossie and McAlmon had simply strolled about sightseeing while passing the time before dinner. The poetry is now flat and casual in tone, and moves with them, conveying their talk and the objects of their attention; and nothing much happens until importunate fingers — tokens of an entire imploring environment — reach out and "the music rouses" suddenly in the mind of the poet.

Penny please! Give me penny please, mister.

Don't give them anything.

. instinctively
one has already drawn one's naked

> wrist away from those obscene fingers
> as in the mind a vague apprehension speaks
> and the music rouses   .

This episode actually precedes the encounter with the
shapeless shape on the bridge, where, as the cry "Wait"
indicates, the poet is at last willing to make contact and
to dance. It represents the poet's first confrontation with
the aboriginal American culture that history has overlaid
with civilization (it reminds one somehow of the "culture" presented in *The Great American Novel*). His
instinctive response to it is not wholly one of revulsion,
though that seems dominant; for, reluctant as he is to
contact it ("one's naked/wrist"— "those obscene fingers"), his "apprehension" is the necessary fear of the
mind that by beginning even vaguely to apprehend, has
roused to the music of poetic inspiration. The image of
the fingers is striking — in itself, and also because it recalls the poet who, in the chapter on night in *A Voyage
to Pagany,* had said that art "begins at the finger nails
— it is these we see and begin with in anguish, the fingers
which annoy us, being always in our sight."[51]

The sightseers evade the beggars by turning into a
bar, and the music is "cut off," barred. Then the walk,
which they shortly resume, is again interrupted, when, to
rest Flossie's (?) feet, they stop at a night club. Here,
to the express pleasure of the poet, a strip tease is about
to begin. It is not much of a show, like everything about
the place; the stripper, whose "cold eyes perfunc-/torily
moan but do not/smile," is "Some worn-out trouper
from/the States." Still the poet is fascinated, for in one
sense she is the anti-poetic, which, Stevens said, was Williams' "spirit's cure."[52] The verse, which now presents
her and the poet's thoughts about her, moves with her
motion, a slow short rhythm:

> There is a fascination
> seeing her shake
> the beaded sequins from
> a string about her hips
>
> She gyrates but it's
> not what you think,
> one does not laugh
> to watch her belly

Accompanying her motions with his eyes and thoughts, the poet dances with her, responds as neither Flossie nor McAlmon does, and again hears the interior music of inspiration:

> The music!
> I like her.   She fits
> the music   .

There are many reasons why she fits the music, though unacknowledged by the poet who himself wonders

> What in the form of an old whore in
> a cheap Mexican joint in Juárez, her bare
> can waggling crazily can be
> so refreshing to me, raise to my ear
> so sweet a tune, built of such slime?

The stripper, of course, is another embodiment of the Beautiful Thing he has pursued. She is America: the "She" Columbus found and with whom De Soto contended; the "marvelous old queen" whom Williams in "The Wanderer" beseeched to grant him the "power to catch something of this day's/Air and sun into your service!"; the "supplying female," the primary source of his fertility and the very stuff he wishes to raise up into art. But there is no longer anything pristine about her; "She" is despoiled, an "old whore," a fallen America that the poet must redeem. She reminds one of Elsie in the poem in *Spring and All* that begins, "The pure products of America/go crazy—" For like the old whore who "in her mockery of virtue/... becomes unaccountably virtuous,"[53] Elsie is

> voluptuous water
> expressing with broken
>
> brain the truth about us—
> her great
> ungainly hips and flapping breasts
>
> addressed to cheap
> jewelry
> and rich young men with fine eyes
>
> as if the earth under our feet
> were
> an excrement of some sky
>
> and we degraded prisoners
> destined
> to hunger until we eat filth[54]

Elsie and the old whore are examples of Williams' "Rabelaisian sanity"—his understanding that "the rare and the fine" come "like everything else from the dirt."[55] From them, as from the bodies of the dancing girls he mentions in *Kora in Hell,* beauty escapes.[56] They are literally flowers of our culture, arising from the sand and rubble of the American ground.[57]

For this reason his association of the old whore with Andromeda is not fortuitous. Both are "presences"; and both are to be saved. The allusion to Andromeda is a good example of Williams' use of the classic, and, by means of associations too subtle to elucidate here, carries one back to the quest-dream that inspired the Keatsian poem of his youth. Like Perseus, who kills the monster associated with the sterility of the land (the desert, the waste land) and the helplessness of the old king (the poet in his old age), Williams is a Messianic hero. By liberating Beautiful Thing he hopes to restore the land.[58]

That we are degraded by the unaccountably virtuous whore is suggested also by the recollection one has on reading the passage on the strip tease of "National Winter Garden" in Hart Crane's *The Bridge,* a poem Williams knew. Here, too, is a dance ("Outspoken buttocks in pink beads") that burlesques our lust and that the poet intends us to recognize as a modern replica of "The Dance," an earlier poem in *The Bridge* in which an Indian brave — and the poet — possesses Pocahontas, the fertile body of America. Both poets use a "mythic" version of American history that was well known in the 1920's;[59] and Crane, in particular, owed much to Williams' large contribution to this myth in *In the American Grain.* But it is not unlikely that Williams, during the composition of *Paterson,* had studied Crane's long poem. When he writes of the old whore's virtue, or later in *Paterson V* on the theme touched on here — that of the virgin and the whore, of purity and spoliation — one thinks of Crane's line on the burlesque queen: "And shall we call her whiter than the snow?" This, in turn, recalls an earlier line affirming that Pocahontas-America "is virgin to the last of men. . . ."[60]

This is the music that the old whore fits, "another music" not the "lying/music," the actual music of her performance and of contemporary culture with which, the poet feels, "This place is rank. . . ." And the music she fits is a music of survival because it is the music of art. The lying music she actually moves to — "this nauseating/prattle about their souls and their loves" — breaks the movement of interior music or perhaps exists simultaneously with it; but, as the poet's response testifies,

the lying music is changed by artifice and art — by
imagination — into something else:

> The bright-colored candy
> of her nakedness lifts her unexpectedly
> to partake of its tune   .[61]

"The bright-colored candy," "those unearthly/greens and
reds," call up the "aniline/red and green candy at the
little booth" and the wonder at this patent token of our
culture: "Do you suppose anyone actually/buys — and
eats the stuff?" Of course they do; the uses to which
Juárez is put proclaim it. And one thinks of Williams' remarks in *The Great American Novel* on the flamboyance
that Vachel Lindsay said was needed to save the American soul, on the seven lively arts, on "Jazz, the Follies,
the flapper in orange and green gown and war-paint of
rouge — impossible frenzies of color in a world that refuses to be drab":

> The imagination will not down. If it is not a dance,
> a song, it becomes an outcry, a protest. If it is not flamboy-
> ance it becomes deformity; if it is not art, it becomes crime.
> Men and women cannot be content, any more than chil-
> dren, with the mere facts of a humdrum life — the imagi-
> nation must adorn and exaggerate life, must give it splen-
> dor and grotesqueness, beauty and infinite depth. And the
> mere acceptance of these things from without is not enough
> — it is not enough to agree and assert when the imagina-
> tion demands for satisfaction creative energy. Flamboyance
> expresses faith in that energy — it is a shout of delight, a
> declaration of richness. It is at least the beginning of art.[62]

In this social-psychological theory, art is a necessity of
survival. The theory explains Williams' own need for
imaginative release as well as the social use for which he
intends his work. This very poem enacts the theory, for
the problem of his survival as an artist — and his need

to survive as an artist — is connected with the survival of his culture. In "The Desert Music," as in *The Bridge*, the poet, however much diminished as a culture-hero, is still needed to save the culture, to lift it up.

The sudden awareness of having for a time moved to this music — and all it implies — is what strikes the poet as they leave the night club to continue their walk; and it forces him to raise those crucial questions which, in the case of both the occasion in the past and the present moment of composition, only a genuine poem can satisfactorily answer:

> am I merely playing the poet? Do I merely invent
> it out of whole cloth? . . .

While he ponders these questions and another question closely related to his practice as a poet — how something vulgar can be poetically fertile ("so sweet a tune, built of such slime?") — they reach the hotel. At this point the form of the verse indicates that the arrival at the hotel and survey of the place, though clearly noted, are part of the poet's "thought," concurrent with it, not wholly the object of it. And the restoration of the freer verse form, the normative verse of the poem, with "Old fashioneds all around?" indicates the poet's emergence from the deeper level of experience; in fact, the question of drinks calls him back from his thought.

. . . I thought   .

> What in the form of an old whore in
> a cheap Mexican joint in Juárez, her bare
> can waggling crazily can be
> so refreshing to me, raise to my ear
> so sweet a tune, built of such slime?

> Here we are. They'll be along any minute.
> The bar is at the right of the entrance,

a few tables opposite which you have to pass
to get to the dining room, beyond.

A foursome, two oversize Americans, no
longer young, got up as cowboys,
hats and all, are drunk and carrying on
with their gals, drunk also,

especially one inciting her man, the
biggest, *Yip ee!* to dance in
the narrow space, oblivious to everything
— she is insatiable and he is trying

stumblingly to keep up with her.
Give it the gun, pardner! *Yip ee!* We
pushed by them to our table, seven
of us. Seated about the room

were quiet family groups, some with
children, eating. Rather a better
class than you notice
on the streets. So here we are. You

can see through into the kitchen
where one of the cooks, his shirt sleeves
rolled up, an apron over
the well-pressed pants of a street

suit, black hair neatly parted,
a tall
good-looking man, is working
absorbed, before a chopping block

Old fashioneds all around?

After the first verse paragraph ("What in the form...."),
the verse goes flat, loses its motion, in keeping with the
fact that the poet sees but does not dance with what he
sees. The experience is passive, which may account for
the lapse from the over-all present tense of the description
("We/pushed by.... Seated about .../were"). Though
the observation follows "the right of way," the poet is

not seeing at the surface of the eye, with the excitement of contact, but from behind it. What he sees, especially the drunken American couples dancing ("carrying on") is another example of the candy culture and lying music that confront him with his role as poet.[63] The oversize Americans got up as cowboys subsume the tall Texans and "Broadway figure" mentioned earlier in the poem; and their dance, while not even the beginning of art, suggests the need for it. Like much that is shoddy in American culture, this dance is framed, in a way Williams employs elsewhere, by an example of a more assured culture, often one of the past: by the quiet family groups, which remind us of the old Indian woman selling candy, and by the true artisan, the cook "working/absorbed," who seems to have begun to compel the poet's attention, recalling as he does men of dignity whom Williams admired, like the Italian fish vendor and the Portuguese stone mason. All of this is part of his thought, which provides the direct continuity from his question, "am I merely playing the poet?" to the questioning statement of the dinner guests, "So this is William/Carlos Williams, the poet   ."

The inquiries of these well-meaning people about the mysterious springs of art, the very thing about which the poet himself has been thinking, accords with the uncertain movement of his inspiration, and for the time being stills the music.

> . . . Why
> does one want to write a poem?
>
> > Because it's there to be written.
>
> Oh. A matter of inspiration then?
>
> > Of necessity.
>
> Oh. But what sets it off?

The questions are not irrelevant; they are the common-places of such occasions. Yet they strike at the core of the matter, as do the poet's answers — because the poem is *there,* in the environment that surrounds him; because he *must* write it to survive. But the questions and answers are never joined (see the spacing) because the poet, though answering truthfully, explains nothing to people who themselves do not know what they are asking — do not know when they say, "A matter of inspiration then?" the agony of inspiration we have been witnessing. ("The reason people marvel at works of art and say: How in Christ's name did he do it? — is that they know nothing of the physiology of the nervous system and have never in their experience witnessed the larger processes of the imagination.")[64] The poet's response, which apparently characterizes the entire dinner, is suggested in lines of acute self-consciousness:

> I am that he whose brains
> are scattered
> aimlessly

Yet these questions, which summarize the action of the poem to this point, are the setting for what follows, when, with dinner done, the poet begins to walk back to El Paso and finds himself almost immediately in contact with the environment

> — and so, on the naked wrist, we feel again
> those insistent fingers   .

With contact the music returns, and he discovers the answer to "what sets it off?"

> . . . so that's
> where the incentive lay, with the annoyance
> of those surprising fingers.

He feels ashamed of his curt replies at dinner and answers now that he writes for

> relief from that changeless, endless
> inescapable and insistent music   .

These lines, in their relentlessness, convey the annoyance he still feels because of the lying music, the crude environment in which he has always lived. Poetry has been for him the relief, the escape, that drink and drugs and women had been for Old Doc Rivers — relief that has sustained his usefulness.

And now, as many times before but always with surprise, the particular conditions of his inspiration are met. The poet has again reached the bridge, and now finds the shapeless shape, which he had introduced at the beginning of the poem. Chronologically, the earlier passage is part of the present episode and might be placed (or reread) after "But what's THAT?" This is the "generative hour" toward which the poem, with increasing intensity, has been leading — the creative moment, filled with terror ("I stood aghast"), that the poem, no recollection in tranquility, subdues and that the tremendous release at the end overcomes.

Probably the recognition of the shapeless shape as "the mother stuff" occurs at the same time as the overwhelming music ("the/*music!*") he associates with Casals:

> the music! the
> *music!* as when Casals struck
> and held a deep cello tone
> and I am speechless   .

> There it sat
> in the projecting angle of the bridge flange
> as I stood aghast and looked at it —
> in the half-light: shapeless or rather returned
> to its original shape, armless, legless,
> headless, packed like the pit of a fruit into
> that obscure corner — or

a fish to swim against the stream — or
a child in the womb prepared to imitate life,
warding its life against
a birth of awful promise. The music
guards it, a mucus, a film that surrounds it,
a benumbing ink that stains the
sea of our minds — to hold us off — shed
of a shape close as it can get to no shape,
a music! a protecting music   .

The music that accompanies this brilliant passage is fittingly that of the cello, a "still, sad music of humanity" such as Wordsworth said he heard, "Not harsh nor grating, though of ample power/To chasten and subdue. . . . " It is fitting because the poet confronts ("looked at it") death as well as birth and *sees* now what he had always acknowledged in the rhythm of descent-ascent: that birth is begotten in death, that to return to the condition of birth is almost to sink down to death.[65] The shape he sees, we know, is that of an old man who has "returned/to [his] original shape," "shed/of a shape close as it can get to no shape"; and though it reminds him of the renewal of life — of the seed, the spawning fish, the child in the womb — it reminds him even more of death. For the seed flourishes at the expense of the fruit, the spawning fish exhausts itself "against the stream," and the child "prepared to imitate life" must be warded "against/a birth of awful promise." Life is now seen not so much as issuing from death as leading to it; and it is this intense awareness of "desert places" that summons the imagination and awakens its equally intense music of survival. The music guards and protects; it surrounds or environs the new life. But in imagery closer to the poet's situation, it is

> a benumbing ink that stains the
> sea of our minds — to hold us off —...

This imagery of the sea belongs with that of *Paterson IV*
(iii), where the poet implores us to turn away from
death:

> I say to you, Put wax rather in your
> ears against the hungry sea
>   it is not our home!

So here the music holds us off by making us both insensi-
tive and blind to death — to those thoughts of death
("If a man die/it is because death/has first/possessed his
imagination")[66] that are our undoing.

When the poet subsequently declares (invokes?) his
vocation —

>   I *am* a poet! I
>   am. I am. I am a poet, I reaffirmed, ashamed

— it is the consequence of both the pitch to which gathering inspiration has raised him and his awareness that he
must be a poet or succumb to his fear of death. To doubt
that he is a poet is for him to doubt the power of poetry,
its efficacy in sustaining life, and for this reason he feels
ashamed. But having affirmed poetry and his faith in life
by reaffirming his vocation — the repeated "I am" calls
the "divine" creative self into being — he is enveloped by
the music and protected in his new life "against/a birth
of awful promise." Now —

> Now the music volleys through as in
> a lonely moment I hear it. Now it is all
> about me. The dance! The verb detaches itself
> seeking to become articulate   .

There is still the terror of creative quickening ("a lonely
moment") but it is overwhelmed by the dominant action
of the "now": the volleying music which surrounds him
and to which he begins to dance. With this access of in-

spiration, "the verb detaches itself," and the poet is ready to make a poem — the very poem he has already put before us.[67]

The relief of this release is expressed by the serene tone and the praise of human powers of the concluding quatrain:

> And I could not help thinking
> of the wonders of the brain that
> hears that music and of our
> skill sometimes to record it.

In this poem the poet has certified that he is a poet by making a poem about the making of poems. He presents those conditions in which the "verb detaches itself," and he gives us the poem by which it becomes "articulate." In treating (and exemplifying) the theme of the imagination's power to make itself its own object, he opens the way to his last poems, especially to the concern for the imagination and its pursuits, which the hunt of the unicorn in *Paterson V* most fully develops. ("It is the imagination/which cannot be fathomed./It is through this hole/we escape . .")[68] And he shows how descent into memory enables an aging poet to do this — why the association of the music with Casals is not fortuitous, why indeed it is associated with the sustenance of the imagination, which it is a function of art to provide, and with those wonderful times in the 1920's he mentions in the foreword of *The Autobiography* when "we'd have been to hear Pablo Casals. Or we'd visit the tapestries at The Cloisters."[69] Having now to reaffirm that he is a poet makes him ashamed because he had known and shared that music, and should live in the assurance of its power. It is the music of Casals and the music of the unicorn tapestries, and that is why, at the end, in speaking of "the wonders of the brain," he celebrates the music of survival.

:: six

"The Desert Music" is about survival not only because it exemplifies the dance by means of which the poet summoned his vital powers, but also because it is about the poet's work — the mastery of chaos, the necessity of form. As an example of the act of renewal, the poem presents an encounter with chaos in which the poet finds in it the inspiration — the energy and conviction of imagination — he needs to rise above it. Form for Williams is organic: it flowers from chaos, rising from the ground of experience by means of the imaginative process of ordering.[1] And this is true of this *poem* in which he depicts the "soul inaugurating a form."[2] But in the *incident* of the poem, the poet does not surmount chaos so much as work through it and find a relation to it that is creative. In the poet's extremity this is enough: to hear the desert music, as the title of the poem indicates, is wonderful enough.

This is so because with advancing age the poet finds threatening the environment upon which he had always relied and must now, to be a poet at all, be assured that what surrounds him is a fertile void rather than Nothing. "Night," in *A Voyage to Pagany,* is immediately followed by a chapter on day — on "the world of form"; and the terror of chaos, which is here the familiar terror before the prospect of creation, is superseded by an invitation to make: "You must begin with nothing, like a river in the morning and make, make new!"[3] The world of the poet in an early poem, "The Farmer," is desolate but not over-whelming, for the time is March, the poet's favorite month, and "the artist figure of/the farmer — compos-ing/— antagonist" looms above the landscape, an un-daunted man against the sky.[4] Williams often despaired of his environment, but not of its power to stir and sus-tain him, and seldom of his imaginative force to make something of it. When, as in this winter season of his life, he despairs of the environment, he is not denying his faith in the organic process but projecting on the en-vironment his fear of diminishing creative power and his presentiment of history — of a social waste land — the later, for a poet of culture, contributing to his sense of the former, and both compounding his sense of self-disintegration. In *Paterson III*, for example, the receding flood leaves only a "fertile (?) mud" in which "most things have lost their/form," and the poet wonders "How to begin to find a shape — to begin to begin again. . . ."[5]

Chaos may be fertile, as Williams knows:

> From disorder (a chaos)
> order grows
> — grows fruitful.
> The chaos feeds it. Chaos
> feeds the tree.[6]

But the chaos, which in so much of the earlier poetry is actually a beneficent richness of life, a swirl of vital pos-sibility, is now not merely disorder but dissolution, not fertile ground but "muck" ("a pustular scum, a decay, a chocking/lifelessness")[7] and desert waste. Once he might say of his forms, as Franco of Cologne says in an early monologue, "I it was that tore you/Out of chaos!"[8] But now, as in the poem praising Sibelius with whom he identifies as artist and culture hero, he considers his art a means of defying the "icy wind," the chaos ("the storm") that enters the mind "where all/good things are secured, written down for love's sake and to defy the devil of emptiness. . . ."[9] Once forms had been a means of ordering life ("From disorder . . ./order grows") and of attaining for the self the large freedom of the imagination; now they had become as well a means of warding the self (in "that obscure corner") against death.

These attitudes toward the environment are at the very center of "The Desert Music":

> Leaving California to return east, the fertile desert,
>   (were it to get water)
> surrounded us, a music of survival, subdued, distant, half
>   heard; we were engulfed
> by it as in the early evening, seeing the wind lift
>   and drive the sand, we
> passed Yuma. All night long, heading for El Paso to
>   meet our friend,
> we slept fitfully. Thinking of Paris, I waked to the tick
>   of the rails. The
> jagged desert   .

At the outset, in keeping with what he had said on his lecture tour about the resources of American art, the desert-chaos is (as in California) fertile ground. It may remind him of the land of youth, of the green land, those gardens that Columbus marveled at; for memory is already awakened, a subdued, distant, half-heard music. Because the land is watered and cared for, survival is possible; there is a music of the ordering imagination. And because this represents for the poet a proper relation to the environment, he feels "surrounded" by it. He knows that the environment, to use the related imagery at the end of the poem, is an enveloping womb warding us from "a birth of awful promise"; that the music of survival, the "protecting music," is both of it and the

imagination, their concord — the measure of their interaction and the token of the consent of the environment
to be taken up (watered) by the imagination and shaped
for human good. But as he moves into another — later
— desert landscape, in fact and in memory, the environment acquires the threatening aspect of his own unrest;
the wind lifts and drives the sand, and he is no longer
surrounded by fertile desert but "engulfed" by sterile
waste. The "jagged desert" that he finally sees in the
daylight of the present is the terrain of his own self.

He is not so much dismayed by the chaos of the external world as by the chaos of his inner world. For he
is not sure, as he was in "The Descent," that in the spaces
memory opens he will find the renewal he seeks. The
poem, significantly, is a descent into memory, and memory is involved in it in a twofold way: the poem treats
the memory of an episode of the recent past, an episode
in which the poet overcomes the chaos of memory and
the accompanying sense of the disintegration of self.
Memory becomes a chaos when the poet, returning East
to visit McAlmon, returns to his own past and recalls
("Thinking of Paris") all that McAlmon had meant to
him and how that visit had been a test of allegiance to
what he proposed to do as an American poet.

The visits, so far apart in time, are curiously similar — and the similarities heighten the differences. Mc-
Almon meets Flossie and Williams in a foreign land,
leads them about, entertains them at dinner. But Mc-
Almon is no longer the "defiant rake-hell of literature"
he had been in Paris but an alcoholic tubercular who
would soon go off to the desert, at Palm Springs, to die;[10]
nor is the poet as confident and resilient and hopeful as
he was then, knowing now, as he wrote in "The Words
Lying Idle," that "the mind is dust also" and the need

to be "appeased against/this dryness and the death implied."[11]

If the spaces of memory threaten disintegration, they also promise redintegration; for they contain, and make present, all that the self has been. The memory of time overcomes time, binds the old self to the new, and is therefore a creative force of the present. And this is what the poet learns by treating memory as the matter of the poem, as the material of his poetic activity. That he fails to recognize Beautiful Thing in the old whore is a consequence of the distress, induced by memory, over his role as poet; but that he responds to her and "dances" with her is a consequence of the continuing imaginative energy that memory, moving profoundly in him, enables him to release. The actual scene has its counterpart in mind, and unconsciously these sallies of the imagination dispel the poet's uneasiness about the environment and restore his confidence in its (her) consent. Moreover, by responding to the old whore he prepares himself for a confrontation at a still deeper level — the confrontation in the "semi-dark" with the shapeless shape of his own disintegrating self. This is the ultimate test of his powers and of his faith in art: to create his life *ab ovo*. And he is helped to meet it successfully when the music he hears evokes from memory the deep cello tone of Casals and he realizes how memory, like art, "kills time."[12] At the end, the music, bringing release, volleys through because the self is once again secure ("I am") and the poet again feels "surrounded" by the world. The "agony of self-realization" is over. He is confident of the "supplying female," now both self and world, and is able to detach the verb. He is ready to make a poem — the poem which in fact he has made — a poem, failing which, as he says in "Asphodel, That Greeny Flower," he was "lost."[13]

"The Desert Music" is representative of almost every aspect of Williams' art: its materials, inspiration, aesthetic, personal, and public ends. The "demonstrationism" — talking within a poem about the problems of the art of poetry — that Vittorio Sereni has noted particularly in "The Desert Music" is not of the sort one frequently finds in Williams' early work, for example, in "To a Solitary Disciple" and "Composition."[14] It enters the poem as part of the poet's meditation, as a fact of his mind and his biography, and is not wholly explicable to an unversed reader. It is his problem, and the demonstration is a desperate one which he makes — must make — more for his own benefit than for our instruction. Nevertheless it is a demonstration of the furthest reach of his art. For what he now means by imitation goes beyond the gift of creativity that the poet shares with nature, a gift he once restricted to the making of objects ("the made poem"); he has learned that the making of poems orders the inner as well as outer chaos and that self-realization by means of art imitates nature in another way — in its power to renew life.

This is the power of art that confirmed Williams' faith in love, the force that he believed death could never beat, and made possible in his closing years his remarkable journey to love. He was always a poet of love, for whom death was the negation of love.[15] What Doc says of his profession in *A Dream of Love* is true of his poetic career: "Life and death. That's the burden of my profession." His dream of love is a dream of life forever renewed, clarified, and intensified by the activity of the imagination — "The thrill," as Doc says, "of a perpetual recovery from an illness."[16] Love and the imagination, Williams claims in "Asphodel, That Greeny Flower," "are of a piece/swift as the light/to avoid destruction."[17]

His encounter with chaos, accordingly, is with darkness and death, with *thanatos,* not with the fertile darkness to which he had been glad to yield, in which he had been "eager to be *soiled,*" but with whatever wills his nothingness; and his victory belongs to *eros,* to all that empowers his creativity. The generative imagery at the end of "The Desert Music" is appropriate. So is the advice of the old poet of *Paterson V:* "Paterson,/Keep your pecker up. . . ."[18]

The affirmation of love is neither as easy nor as sentimental as we usually believe it to be. Williams earned it, honestly and courageously, in the face of death — his and the world's. Or perhaps we should say that he maintained it: that rejoicing "more than other men in the spirit of life that is in him" and having "great faith in a seed," it was his constitutionally, to be defended throughout a long and troubled lifetime.[19] The shapeless shape that portends death is in fact egg-shaped and reminds the poet of seed and spawn and embryo; the images are double because he knows that death begets life, is the sacrifice of life that engenders the seed. To this end — the poem invites this reading of his career — he had been willing to give his life; poems were his seeds, contributions to the renewal of life in our time. And this poem, which describes the difficult making of a poem still to be made, is a supreme testimony of this faith, for in the fertile moment at the end — in both his own creative readiness to undergo the labor of art and his respect for all human effort toward life — he is upholding the great declaration of faith in organic results he had made in "Rogation Sunday":

> O let the seeds be planted
> and the worry and the unrest be invited!
> Let that which is to come

of the weather and our own weakness
be accepted!

Let work mate with fertility
the man and the soil join to produce
a world, a world of blade and blossom!
We believe! We believe
in the wonder of continuous revival,
the ritual of the farm.

This is our world and this
is our message to the world and to each other:
Let the seed be planted, the man
and the soil be ploughed equally
by the joy in the planting —
that the grass, the grasses that bear
the seeds: oat, rye and corn
and other yield
speak their message of revival and thrive
by our labor this Maytime.

Coda:

Who shall reap the harvest?
To whom shall the praise be given?
No man — but all men together in love
and devotion. There is no other harvest
and no other praise!
O let the seeds be planted and the rain
and the sun and the moon add their wonder.[20]

In "The Desert Music" the poet renews his faith
and rebuilds the foundations of his world. He looks intently at the self and plumbs his own resources. The
harmony of the self and its relation to the world have
been restored — and the possibility of art, order, and
culture, for this, too, is what the music heralds as it
breaks through the wastes of death, self, and civilization.
To the question he asked in *Spring and All* —"What

would have happened in a world . . . lit by the imagination"—this poem suggests an answer.[21] And it is both more affirmative than *Paterson IV* and more convincing.

"The Desert Music" is one of Williams' answers to *The Waste Land*. "Asphodel, That Greeny Flower," another celebration of the imagination, incorporates motifs of Eliot's poem in its own affirmation of light; in it Williams keeps his promise to contest Eliot to his last breath:

> ... there is as much to say
> and more
> for the one side
> and that not the darker
> which John Donne
> for instance
> among many men
> presents to us.[22]

But he was also thinking of Eliot at the time he was composing "The Desert Music." In the letter to Frank L. Moore, in which he comments on imitation, he mentions Eliot in the context of urgent considerations of death and invention.

Death, and how to approach it, preoccupy him. Death "claps you between its hands like a flying moth, and you are done"; it "dominates our world." And its presence is so real to him ("too real for me") that he cannot dodge it or find refuge from it in "myth" ("the often-repeated"), in the entertainment of art, in dogma, or in the church. "You see what [Thomas] Merton did," he remarks scornfully, "became a half-assed monk." And of Eliot: "Or what Mr. Eliot [he is usually Mr. Eliot to Williams] did—went on writing books! Books! as if they had some hope of them." (He is not impugning writing but the activity of writing which may be evasive—and also the repetition suggested by "went on.") For himself he wants the serenity and clarity that he finds in the *Iliad,* that "pure invention" in which "the air is clear [and] there is no interested fog between the words and the senses." "We have a carved East Indian mask," he explains. "I saw it last night while I was listening to some music. It came to life, complacent before death, complete peace. It was a lesson to me — and no dogma to soften the blow. It had the peace before violent death that is in the *Iliad,* and the consciousness, the complete consciousness, before it that is in the heroes of Greek legend. . . ."[23]

Having been won in the face of death, the serenity of the poet, at the close of "The Desert Music," is of this kind.

> And I could not help thinking
> of the wonders of the brain that
> hears that music and of our
> skill sometimes to record it.

The terror he has known and overcome is not the seasonal terror of growth expressed in "Portrait of the Author," where

> . . . coldly the birch leaves are opening one by one.
> Coldly I observe them and wait for the end.
> And it [the terror] ends.[24]

Renewal, now, is not for him a possibility within the cycles of the seasons, nor is it prompted so much, as in this early poem, by changes in the external world. Now renewal involves the "wonders of the brain," the imitation by which "we . . . become nature, and so invent an object which is an extension of the process." "The Desert Music" ends with the poet's serene thoughts — thoughts about the representative human powers of the artist — because he has, in composing this poem, made a "pure invention."

Williams had always been a proponent of the new, of forms, as he said in the *Briarcliff Quarterly* letter, "generated, invented, today direct from the turmoil itself. . . ." In this letter, one of his many answers to Eliot and Pound, he explained that "when my friends went abroad I stayed here pitting myself against a chaos in my attempts to do what to me was the artist's greatest and most difficult task, to wrest from society . . . new worlds of art."[25] It is likely that he still remembered Eliot's comments, in the introduction to Pound's *Selected Poems,* on the impossibility of invention ("When I say 'invent', I should use inverted commas, for invention would be irreproachable if it were possible") and on the nature of originality ("There is a shallow test which holds that the original poet goes direct to life, and the derivative poet to 'literature' ").[26] In any case, he stood by invention.[27] "The Desert Music" is such an invention — a new complex form of high order — in which the formal achievement, in terms of the cultural meaning of the poem, represents the poet's fulfilled responsibility to America. ("America is lost. Ah Christ, Ah Christ that night should come so soon," he had written in *The Great American Novel.* "And the reason is that no American poet . . . has taken the responsibility upon his own person.")[28] And the poem warrants the faith in invention that informs so much of the late poetry and that Williams declares in "Deep Religious Faith":

> Past death
> > past rainy days
> > > or the distraction
> > of lady's-smocks all silver-white;
> > > beyond the remote borders
> > > > of poetry itself
> > if it does not drive us,
> > > it is vain

Invention ("It is what in life drives us") is the organic necessity:

> All that which makes the pear ripen
> or the poet's line
> come true!
> Invention is at the heart of it.

And to have forgotten this is the shame of "our poets":

> they have forgot
> the flower!
> which goes beyond all
> laboratories!
> They have quit the job
> of invention. The
> imagination has fallen asleep
> in a poppy-cup.[29]

In dismissing invention, Eliot dismissed the very thing for which he was acclaimed by F. R. Leavis, who, having set down his test of poets ("To invent techniques that shall be adequate to the ways of feeling, or modes of experience, of adult, sensitive moderns"), said of him that "he has made a new start, and established new bearings." No one will deny this. And the same may be said of Williams. For in addition to passing the test of "technical originality . . . inseparable from the rare adequacy of mind, sensibility and spirit that it vouches for" and of showing "himself to have been fully alive in our time," he demonstrated, in a time of despair, "what hopeful men can do."[30]

:: notes

ACKNOWLEDGMENTS AND KEY TO ANNOTATIONS

For the convenience of the reader and by way of acknowledgment for permission to reprint passages from the writings of William Carlos Williams, the following chronologically arranged list of the poet's work is appended. A shorthand key to titles is indicated in the margin.

KH   *Kora in Hell: Improvisations* (San Francisco, City Lights, 1957). Published originally by The Four Seas Company, Boston, 1920.

SA   *Spring and All* (Dijon, Contact Publishing Co., 1923).

GAN   *The Great American Novel* reprinted in *American Short Novels*, ed. R. P. Blackmur (New York, Thomas Y. Crowell Co., 1960), pp. 307-343. Originally published by Contact Editions, Paris, 1923.

IAG   *In the American Grain* (New York, New Directions, 1956). Originally published by Albert & Charles Boni, New York, 1925.

VP   *A Voyage to Pagany* (New York, The Macaulay Co., 1928).

WM   *White Mule* (Norfolk, Conn., New Directions, 1937).

ITM   *In the Money* (Norfolk, Conn., New Directions, 1940).

P   *Paterson* (New York, New Directions, 1963). This is the paperback edition of Books I-V, published respectively in 1946, 1948, 1949, 1951, 1958.

CLP   *The Collected Later Poems* (New York, New Directions, 1963). This is a revised edition of the book, originally published in 1950. Copyright 1950 by William Carlos Williams. "Rogation Sunday" reprinted by permission of New Directions Publishing Corporation.

CEP   *The Collected Earlier Poems* (New York, New Directions, 1951). Copyright 1938 by William Carlos Williams. "The Right of Way" and a portion of "To Elsie" reprinted by permission of New Directions Publishing Corporation.

A   *The Autobiography of William Carlos Williams* (New York, Random House, Inc., 1951).

BU   *The Build-Up* (New York, Random House, Inc., 1952).

SE   *Selected Essays* (New York, Random House, Inc., 1954).

SL   *Selected Letters of William Carlos Williams,* ed. John C. Thirlwall (New York, McDowell, Obolensky, 1957).

IWW   *I Wanted to Write a Poem: The Autobiography of the Works of a Poet,* reported and edited by Edith Heal (Boston, Beacon Press, 1958).

ML   *Many Loves and Other Plays* (New York, New Directions, 1961).

FD   *The Farmers' Daughters: The Collected Stories* (New York, New Directions, 1961).

PB   *Pictures from Brueghel and Other Poems* (New York, New Directions, 1962). Copyright 1954, 1959 by William Carlos Williams. Contains *The Desert Music* (1954) and *Journey to Love* (1955). "The

Desert Music," "The Dance," and a portion of "Asphodel, That Greeny Flower" reprinted by permission of New Directions Publishing Corporation.

SECTION ONE

1. *IWW*, 89. Vittorio Sereni, who translated "The Desert Music," observes that "I gained less satisfaction from translating this poem than others of his, but even so I wonder how right Williams is in calling the other poems 'more important' than the one that names the volume." "W.C.W.: An Italian View," *Prairie Schooner*, XXXVIII (Winter, 1964-65), 308.

2. *SL*, 301, 302.

3. *A*, 136, 161. It is more likely that he read at an exhibition of the Society of Independent Artists than at the Armory Show. See Constance Rourke, *Charles Sheeler: Artist in the American Tradition* (New York, Harcourt, Brace and Company, 1938), p. 50.

4. *SL*, 304-305.

5. *SL*, 302.

6. *SL*, 298-300.

7. *SL*, 300, 301.

8. *IWW*, 88; *SL*, 302.

9. *Botteghe Oscure*, No. 8 (1951), p. 318. The poem was also published in *Origin*, VI (Summer, 1952), 65-75; and this text was used in the mock-up of the book.

SECTION TWO

1. *IWW*, 88.

2. *SL*, 261.

3. *CLP*, 253.

4. *McAlmon and the Lost Generation*, ed. Robert E. Knoll (Lincoln, University of Nebraska Press, 1962), p. 243.

5. *CEP*, 229. This is birth. In "By the Road to the Contagious Hospital," he writes of the sprouting grasses:

> They enter the new world naked,
> cold, uncertain of all
> save that they enter. All about them
> the cold, familiar wind —

(*CEP*, 241.) And in *White Mule*, he writes of his wife Flossie's birth: "She entered, as Venus from the sea, dripping. The air enclosed her, touching, waking her. If Venus did not cry aloud after release from the pressures of that sea-womb, feeling the new and lighter flood springing in her chest, flinging out her arms —this one did. . . . She let out three convulsive yells. . . ." Though Williams suggests that release is not entirely joyful, the midwife thinks otherwise: "Stop that crying, said Mrs. D, you should be glad to get outa that hole." (P. 1.)

6. "An Approach to the Poem," *English Institute Essays, 1947* (New York, Columbia University Press, 1948), p. 58.

7. Of his aged mother, whose passion for life he shared, he says:

> . . . you want so wildly to escape
> as I wish also
> to escape and leap into chaos

And he gives her brandy because it kindles life —

> that fertile darkness
> in which passion mates —
> reflecting
> the lightnings of creation —

(*CEP*, 375-378.)

8. Night is what he was later to call the "supplying female," the chaos of a living society; and it is the body of America, a fertile and terrifying source of new forms. See "Letter to an Australian Editor," *Briarcliff Quarterly*, III (October, 1946), 208. Against book-begotten art, Williams put the sexually created; as Charles Sheeler succinctly said, "In the newborn child he finds the seedling of all living forms." "In a Handful of Pebbles," *ibid.*, p. 204.

9. *SE*, 18.

10. *KH*, 50. And this, at the end of his life, he says in *Paterson V*, is all he knows:

> . . . to dance to a measure
> contrapuntally,
>   Satyrically, the tragic foot.

(*P*, 278.)

11. *VP*, 249-250. This experience is especially relevant to much that characterizes Williams. Consider, for example, his remark to Kenneth Burke on his return from Europe in 1924: "No creed but clarity. Work in, in, in. . . ." (*SL*, 65.) Or this line from "Portrait of the Author": "Black is split at once into flowers. . . ." which finds, as perhaps all flower references in Williams' work do, an echo in the prayer in *Paterson*, where the poet says that "The world spreads/for me like a flower opening." (*CEP*, 218; *P*, 93.) And consider also the comments on rescuing

oneself, on preserving the "unblemished area of the first revelation hidden in his [the child's] secret heart, [where] he will live and most beautifully blossom." (*SE*, 270.)

12. *P*, 48.

13. *VP*, 281.

14. Since the master rhythm of Williams' life is descent-ascent, it is possible to chart many changes from book to book in the course of his work, as Richard Macksey does in " 'A Certainty of Music': Williams' Changes" in *William Carlos Williams: A Collection of Critical Essays*, ed. J. Hillis Miller (Englewood Cliffs, N.J., Prentice-Hall, Inc., 1966), pp. 132-147. I have discussed only those changes I consider of major importance.

15. See *A*, 343, written at this time, where Williams, in reference to Pound and covertly in reference to himself, speaks of confinement (and birth), and of the life in the seed of the poem.

16. *IWW*, 80ff. "The Descent," the sole object of Williams' comments on *Paterson II*, is reprinted here. One remark is noteworthy: "Several years afterward in looking over the thing I realized that I had hit upon a device . . . which I could not name when I wrote it."

SECTION THREE

1. *ML*, 102. In the foreword of *The Autobiography*, Williams speaks of the "burning inside me" that demanded outlet, of "something growing inside me demand[ing] reaping"; "I would be like a woman at term," and delivered by writing, he felt "cleansed of that torment. . . ." Most of his metaphors of the psychology of creation are here.

2. *A*, 288.

3. *A*, xii. Kenneth Burke has written wonderfully on this theme in his memorial essay on Williams, reprinted in *William Carlos Williams: A Collection of Critical Essays*, pp. 50-61.

4. *SE*, 78. The function Joyce performs is comparable to that of the Viennese physicians praised in *A Voyage to Pagany*.

5. *A*, 288. The account of Columbus' discovery in *In the American Grain* ends with Columbus serenely walking in the gardens of the New World "among the trees which was the most beautiful thing which I had ever seen. . . ." This is the source of the phrase "Beautiful Thing"; the concept, however, appears earlier in other guises.

Williams' quest was romantic but not visionary. Having begun to write under the influence of Keats, he learned, it seems, what Keats does in *The Fall of Hyperion*, that the poet is " 'A humanist, physician to all men' " and that

'The poet and the dreamer are distinct,

. . . .

'The one pours out a balm upon the World,
'The other vexes it. . . .'
(Canto I, ll. 190, 199-202.)

6. *SA*, 27. A poem is a form of (the) imagination.

7. *SE*, 62, 72.

8. *SL*, 122, 150, 169.

9. *SL*, 216-217; Hartley and his "need" are warmly treated in *The Autobiography*; see also *SE*, xvi.

10. *SL*, 202, 215.

11. *CLP*, 59, 7.

12. *SL*, 214.

13. *The Case of Ezra Pound*, ed. Charles Norman (New York, The Bodley Press, 1948), pp. 47-54. Williams made this point about Pound as early as 1922, about Eliot as late as 1948. See *SE*, 35, 289.

14. *SE*, 212.

15. *SL*, 192.

16. "Notes Towards a Definition of Culture," *Partisan Review*, XI (Spring, 1944), 145-157. R. P. Blackmur, Clement Greenberg, William Phillips, and I. A. Richards replied to this essay in *Partisan Review* (Summer, 1944); Dwight Macdonald replied in *Politics*. See John C. Thirlwall, "William Carlos Williams as Correspondent," *The Literary Review*, I (Autumn, 1957), 18-19.

17. *A*, 59-60.

18. Open, organic form is central to Williams' notions of both culture and poetry, and measure in poetry is a cultural issue. In "Against the Weather" (1939), he speaks of a measure that "must be one of more trust, greater liberty, than has been permitted in the past. It must be an open formation." Against this, he notes, there was "the countering cry of Order! Order! [absolute order] . . . That was the time of the new Anglo-Catholicism." (*SE*, 212.) In his view, developed especially in his historical studies, liberty must replace authority, the local the distant (absentee), the particular and sensual the abstract, the relative the absolute (with the backing of Einstein). All are aspects of the "newness," the make-it-new of modernism, which America, historically favored, has the special opportunity to advance.

19. *SE*, 147, 148ff., 157, 210; *SL*, 214. This essay, Williams' tribute to Alfred Stieglitz, represents the cultural goals of a generation that includes Benton MacKaye, who championed the

resources of the indigenous environment in *The New Exploration* (1928), and Randolph Bourne, who envisioned a "trans-national America." The citation from Frank Lloyd Wright, who also shared these views of culture, is from *An Autobiography* (New York, Duell, Sloan and Pearce, 1943), p. 312, where the word "indigenous" is added to the original text of the 1932 edition. Williams may have read the first edition or perhaps have heard Wright's Princeton lectures of 1930. In any case, having a brother who was an architect, he was familiar with the language of architecture and had an architectural notion of poetic composition.

20. These conceptions of culture have figured prominently in contemporary criticism. Consider, for example, Karl Shapiro, who equates "Culture poetry" with modern poetry and defines it as "poetry in reverse; it dives back into the historical situation, into culture, instead of flowering from it." *In Defense of Ignorance* (New York, Random House, 1960), pp. 21-22. And consider Denis Donoghue, who cites and seriously appreciates Williams' views of culture, but being "of Eliot's party" cannot accept a "Grammar of Culture without benefit of Clergy. . . ." "For a Redeeming Language," *Twentieth Century,* CLXIII (June, 1958), 532-542. For the depth and range of Williams' concern with American culture, see Joseph Evans Slate, "William Carlos Williams' Image of America" (unpublished Ph.D. dissertation, University of Wisconsin, 1957).

A poet of culture (all that immediately environs us) is one who in his art responds to the living needs of his time and tries to make his art a force in the situation of his time. Eliot, Pound, and Williams try to do this; all are poets of culture. But Eliot and Pound offer Culture as a solution to the problems of culture; and each has a doctrine, the one religious, the other economic. Williams, however, offers only poetry: the imaginative action of men in contact with their environment.

21. *SL,* 224-227. See *Paterson I,* "Preface":

> To make a start,
> out of particulars
> and make them general. . . .

22. *SE,* 21.

23. *Sewanee Review,* LV (Summer, 1947), 500-503. Perceptively, he compares *Paterson* to *The Prelude,* a great work of autobiography — a poem about "the growth of a poet's mind." He says that "Paterson is Williams' life, and Williams is what makes Paterson alive." In a letter to McAlmon, Williams de-

scribed *Paterson* as "an account, a psychologic-social panorama of a city treated as if it were a man. . . ." *SL,* 216.

24. *Partisan Review,* XIII (September-October, 1946), 488-500.

25. *SL,* 233.

26. *SL,* 250.

27. "Ezra Pound," *Poetry,* LXVIII (September, 1946), 326-338; Dillon on p. 325.

28. See *SE,* 24, and especially "Caviar and Bread Again: A Warning to the New Writer," *SE,* 102-104. "When I was at the University of Pennsylvania, around 1905, I used to argue with Pound. I'd say 'bread' and he'd say 'caviar.' It was a sort of simplification of our positions. . . ." Quoted by Harvey Breit, *The Writer Observed* (Cleveland and New York, World Publishing Company, 1956), p. 100.

29. *Briarcliff Quarterly,* III (October, 1946), 205-208. This letter is a coda to the introduction to *The Wedge;* its social and political cast reflects the war and its assurance reflects the successful early work on *Paterson.* Louis Martz, who has considered it in another, though related, context, points out the relation between Williams' notion of mind-begetting-mind and Eliot's notion of tradition and the individual talent. See "On the Road to *Paterson," The Poem of the Mind* (New York, Oxford University Press, 1966), pp. 145-146.

. This issue of sources and nurture is one of long standing in discussions of American culture. Williams considers it historically when he sees the American Revolution as an essentially cultural conflict between "present reliance on the prevalent conditions of place and the overriding of an unrelated authority." (*SE,* 143.) This view comprehends Herder's notion that the artist should turn for nurture to folk rather than literary sources, a notion still current in the critical work of the generation of Van Wyck Brooks and most eloquently stated by Constance Rourke in *The Roots of American Culture* (New York, Harcourt, Brace and Company, 1942). Miss Rourke lays down "the principle that the American artist cannot take off from the same points of departure as the European artist" and observes that "the center of growth of any distinctive culture is to be found within the social organism and is created by peculiar and irreducible social forces." (Pp. 291, 284.) Appropriate to this discussion is Whitman's statement in the Preface to the 1855 edition of *Leaves of Grass:* "The direct trial of him who would be the greatest poet is today. . . . If he does not attract his own land body and soul . . . and plunge his semitic muscle into its merits and demerits [etc.]. . . ." (See *KH,* 72, where Williams speaks of the poet's "phallus-like argument.") And there is also Thoreau's detailed account of the organic growth of the mind, which ends: "There are minds which so have their roots in other minds as in the womb of nature, — if, indeed, most are not such?!" (*The Writings of Henry David Thoreau, Journal,* II, ed. Bradford Torrey [Boston and New York, Houghton Mifflin and Company, 1906], pp. 201-205.)

An observation on mind-begotten art of interest to the contemporary cultural situation is the following: androgynously begotten art, Williams believes, explains "why women are generally considered only accessory to the arts; it explains also the philosophic basis for the present homosexual diversion in New York. . . ." (*Briarcliff Quarterly,* 205.) Here perhaps is the reason for Cress's anger in *Paterson II* and for Williams' disgust with the homosexuality of the beat generation. (See Walter Sutton, "A Visit with William Carlos Williams," *Minnesota Review,* I (Spring, 1961), 324.)

30. "On the poet devolves the most vital function of society: to recreate it. . . ." (*SE,* 103.)

31. Williams' pun on "credit" must be acknowledged and the equally serious pun of

> Money: Joke
> could be wiped out
> at stroke
> of pen
> and was when
> gold and pound were
> devalued

(*P,* 217.)

32. In *Paterson V,* Pound no longer is accorded this virtue. He is quoted as saying, "let the young   educ   the young." (P. 254.)

33. *SE,* 21; *P,* 234.

34. *P,* 208.

35. This relationship is treated again in a different key in the Phyllis-Paterson episodes of *Paterson IV;* it was first depicted in *The Great American Novel* (1923).

36. "Some Notes Towards an Autobiography," *Poetry,* LXXII (June, 1948), 147-155; (August, 1948), 264-270; LXXIV (May, 1949), 94-111.

37. *SL,* 275.

38. *CLP,* 106, 119, 122.

39. Quoted in John C. Thirlwall, "William Carlos Williams' 'Paterson,' " *New Directions 17* (1961), 254.

40. "View of 3 Poets," *Partisan Review,* XVIII (November, 1951), 698-700; reprinted in *Poetry and the Age* (New York, Alfred A. Knopf, 1953), pp. 250-265.

41. *IWW,* 79.

42. Conrad Aiken calls "The Wanderer" the "ur-Paterson." *A Reviewer's ABC* (London, W. H. Allen, 1961), p. 385.

43. This high conception of the poet's role was one of the ideas of the nineteenth century still powerfully current in the period ended by World War I. It was vigorously set forth in Van Wyck Brooks's *America's Coming-of-Age* (New York, B. W. Huebsch, 1915) and *Letters and Leadership* (New York, H. W. Huebsch, 1918). Even when poets could not accept the political responsibility Brooks attached to this role — or for the very reason that they could not — they assimilated the sense of power he associated with art to the notion of poet of culture. Brooks himself, without losing the force of the idea, moved from politics to culture. Pound, Eliot, and Williams were his contemporaries; these were their formative years.

44. *P,* 132.

45. *P,* 30-31.

46. In November, 1943, Williams, in writing James Laughlin about his reading of Forster's *The Longest Journey,* glossed the meaning of the title of a later book of poems: "the journey back to love, the longest journey. . . ." "Four Unpublished Letters by William Carlos Williams," *The Massachusetts Review,* III (Winter, 1962), 293-294.

SECTION FOUR

1. *SL,* 271. Williams speaks of "the diary of our trip to France 1924-25" and this may be exactly what it was. Though the date above is inaccurate, the account in *The Autobiography* is limited pretty much to France. Of the diary he said: "Strange to read it now (tho God knows I didn't take time to read it this afternoon)."

2. According to James Dickey, a poet's rating may be judged by his place in anthologies. Rexroth's poem first appeared in the Williams' issue of *Briarcliff Quarterly.*

3. *SL,* 284; *A,* 4; *IWW,* 26. For Thirlwall, see "William Carlos Williams' 'Paterson,' " *New Directions 17,* p. 257. Williams told Sister M. Bernetta Quinn in 1951, in commending her article on *Paterson,* that "your reference . . . to *The Wanderer*

astonishes me. I had no idea that anyone would take the trouble to investigate my origins." (*SL*, 309.) For the passages of *Paterson V*, see pp. 270, 271, 277 (where "You young people/think you know everything" is a variation of lines in "The Last Words of My English Grandmother," published in 1920, and recalled in Chapter 15 of *The Great American Novel,* published in 1923).

4. *SL*, 285-286. In the Preface to *Paterson I*, Williams admits his "defective means." One of the few critics to appreciate Williams' critical writing was Conrad Aiken, who followed closely the work done by the poets of his generation. In 1934, in a review of *Collected Poems*, he noted that "like Eliot (who is in other respects his antithesis), he seems to have developed, simultaneously, a very individual style and a formidable critical awareness with which to defend it." "The Well Worn Spirit," *New Republic,* LXXVIII (April 18, 1934), 289-291; reprinted in *A Reviewer's ABC,* pp. 380-383.

5. *SL*, 295. See "Chicory and Daisies," *CEP,* 122, especially the concluding lines:

> the sky goes out
> if you should fail.

6. "William Carlos Williams' Rich, Sprawling Memoirs," *New York Herald Tribune Book Review,* September 16, 1951, p. 1; reprinted in *A Reviewer's ABC,* pp. 383-386.

7. *SL*, 287-288.

8. *IWW,* 77-78, 84. Congress investigated the award by The Fellows in American Letters of the Library of Congress of the Bollingen Prize to Ezra Pound in 1949, and the Library was forced to cancel all future awards. Williams had been made a fellow, after the prize was awarded. He was appointed Consultant in Poetry in 1952, but because of agitation against him did not take the appointment. The account in *IWW* fuses both incidents.

9. *A*, 317-319. Robert Lowell, whose writing on Williams is sensitive to the poet's response to his later years, dedicated to Williams Villon's "The Great Testament." This poem, one of Williams' favorites, begins:

> Where are those gallant men
> I ran with in my youth?

Imitations (London, Faber and Faber, 1962), p. 8.

10. *IWW,* 86. The phrase is especially meaningful because he had had, in 1952 and later, some psychoanalytic treatment. See *SL*, 314; "Four Unpublished Letters of William Carlos Williams," *Massachusetts Review,* p. 296.

11. *A Reviewer's ABC,* p. 384.

12. *IWW*, 9-10.

13. *Opus Posthumous* (London, Faber and Faber, 1959), p. 173; *SL*, 194. In an early review of his work, Marianne Moore wrote: "Despite Dr. Williams' championing of the school of ignorance, or rather of no school but experience, there is in his work the authoritativeness, the wise silence which knows schools and fashions well enough to know that completeness is further down than professional intellectuality and modishness can go." Reprinted from *Contact* (1921) in *William Carlos Williams: A Collection of Critical Essays*, p. 39.

14. *SL*, 113.

15. "Agh, Old Ez," Williams replies in an interview; "A pain in the ass. . . . He wants me to be known as a more or less uneducated man." (Sutton, "A Visit with William Carlos Williams," *Minnesota Review*, p. 314.) In the *Briarcliff Quarterly* letter he writes: "To Ezra, a friend, — but regretfully rather a backward pupil. Pupil is the key word, he wants to teach me. Otherwise what can I possibly amount to?" (P. 206.)

16. Eliot, "Ezra Pound," *Poetry*, p. 337; Sutton, "A Visit with William Carlos Williams," *Minnesota Review*, p. 317. In explaining Williams' notion of contact, Kenneth Burke said: "Contact might be said to resolve into the counterpart of Culture, and Williams becomes thereby one of our most distinguished Neanderthal men." "Heaven's First Law," *The Dial*, LXXII (February, 1922), 197-200.

17. He was educated in Switzerland and in a New York City high school comparable to a lycée. He studied medicine at the University of Pennsylvania and later at Leipzig and Vienna. He published translations in French and Spanish. ("I knew a damn sight more French than he [Pound] did.") (Sutton, "A Visit with William Carlos Williams," *Minnesota Review*, p. 314.) In "Seventy Years Deep," a short autobiographical piece in *Holiday*, XVI (November, 1954), 54-55, 78, Williams says: "No one — and I am not the first to say it — ever made a mark in the world of letters without a solid background of good reading."

18. *CLP*, 39, 65; *A*, 44, 390-391. The attitude toward his detractors in these poems is similar to that in *The Autobiography*.

19. *A*, 3; see also *SL*, 328-331, where Williams tells the episode of the drum in the context of measure. Eliot remarks in *The Use of Poetry and the Use of Criticism* (London, Faber and Faber, 1933), p. 155: "Poetry begins, I dare say, with a savage beating a drum. . . ."

20. *SL*, 286, 289-290. The quotation about Ulysses, which is particularly significant for the end of the poem, Book IV, is a

part of a discussion that indicates a thematic connection with Book V ("Today we give ourselves more easily than Ulysses did and are not destroyed by it: we cure syphilis in a week by penicillin!"). In *A,* 392, Ulysses is fittingly replaced by Whitman. The *Odyssey* and *Iliad* also underlie the work of Joyce and Pound, with whom Williams wishes to stand. Williams' classicism is best defined by Constance Rourke in *Charles Sheeler: Artist in the American Tradition.*

21. *Opus Posthumous,* p. 165.

22. *A,* xi.

23. *A,* 222, 228; *ML,* 200.

24. *ML,* 200; *A,* 222.

25. *P,* 219.

26. *ML,* 201. Though Flossie is the Venus of *White Mule,* Williams says in *The Autobiography* that she was "no Venus de Milo." (P. 130.) In "Asphodel, That Greeny Flower," his petition to Flossie for forgiveness, he admits that "All women are not Helen,/I know that, but have Helen in their hearts," and is able, imaginatively, to suggest the reconciliation he seeks, when, confessing that he regrets most the end of his word-making (words are his breath of life as this poem to extend it shows), he says, merging Flossie with Beautiful Thing:

> For in spite of it all,
>> all that I have brought on myself,
>>> grew that single image
> that I adore
>> equally with you
>> and so
> it brought us together.

(*PB,* 159, 169.) Williams depicts the difficulties with Flossie over this poetic pursuit in early works like *Kora in Hell* and *The Great American Novel,* in the story "To Fall Asleep," in the plays *Many Loves* and *A Dream of Love,* in the essay "The Basis of Faith in Art," and in various poems. Only *passim* would fully index this theme.

27. *PB,* 182. Here, as in other late poems, there is a sensuousness hitherto absent. The world of the poet is now internal and what would have been expressed earlier in terms of ascent is now expressed in terms of descent, as penetration and diffusion in the sensuous ground of the self. Williams was never more sensuous. The descent to memory, which contributes so much to these poems, released a new self. This (and the fact that these materials permitted him to survive as an artist and to live in his very life while he used it up) may account for

the remarkable vigor and sense of life that accompany his pursuit of the past. This homecoming to love, and Flossie's place in it, is prefigured in *The First President* (1936), where Washington's life is a parable of Williams'. When the defeated President retires — gives up his public role — "Martha [his "protector"] takes him to herself again for a few years. And so the cycle is completed." (*ML*, 312.)

28. *SL*, 293. "Biography" is a significant slip, suggesting more detachment and artfulness than is possible in autobiography.

29. *A Reviewer's ABC*, p. 384.

30. *A*, 216-217.

31. Williams writes of Shakespeare: "This is the sort of person who lives in one place, having no need to move his carcass in order to keep alive. It is the imagination that travels: Pattern of the more serious interval between the serious travel of being born and dying. How shall a man rival that journey . . . ?" (*SE*, 55.) This is the essential drift of "Seventy Years Deep," *Holiday*; the most significant thing about this article is its title.

32. *IAG*, 216, 225. Benjamin T. Spencer points out the Platonic aspect of this locality — and one thinks of Williams' "secret gardens of the self" in connection with it. "Doctor Williams' American Grain," *Tennessee Studies in Literature*, VIII (1963), 1-16.

33. *SA*, 36; see *FD*, 89-90; *IAG*, 213. Williams' view of Poe enables him to connect Poe and Whitman, who are usually seen as representing the extreme positions of our literary tradition. For a contemporary essay correcting Williams, see Laura Riding, "Jamais Plus," *Transition*, VII (October, 1927), 139-156.

34. Williams' tribute is in *John Marin* (Berkeley, University of California Press, 1956). Paul Rosenfeld, in a book of essays including one on Williams, said that "Marin is fast in American life like a tough and fibrous apple tree lodged and rooted in good ground." *Port of New York* (New York, Harcourt, Brace and Company, 1924), p. 153.

35. *ITM*, 155-157; *WM*, 197-198.

36. *PB*, 33.

37. For other autobiographical accounts see *SL*, *A Dream of Love*, *BU*, Preface to *SE*.

38. *A Reviewer's ABC*, p. 386. Aiken's broken childhood may have made him receptive to Williams. Williams began the composition of *The Autobiography* with what he called "The Middle Years" and went on to "The Last Phase." Then, in January, 1951, he returned to his early years and filled out

the notes he had published in *Poetry*. See Williams' manuscripts, Yale University Library.

39. See *GAN,* Chapter 5: "So they lay in the little brook and let the cold water run up their bare bellies."

The necessity of ritual renewal in *The Autobiography* is established by the struggles, defeats, and family disasters that precede it.

40. *The Writings of Henry David Thoreau,* III, 90. See also, *A,* 239, for Williams' trip to the Maine Woods.

41. *SE,* 26. This is an early citation of a frequently expressed idea. It is also a correlative of his physical need for movement. In "The Wanderer," where, following Whitman, he stands at the prow of the ferry, it is also expressed by a Whitman-like soaring flight.

42. The publication of *The Waste Land* is for Williams representative of an aspect of the cultural situation that Frederick Hoffman has noted, that "in the twenties the separation between native culture and a sophisticated culture which had its roots in Western Europe was to become greater than ever." Review of J. A. Moreau, *Randolph Bourne* in *American Literature,* XXXVIII (January, 1967), 578.

43. In "A Poet Remembers," a tribute to Paul Rosenfeld, Williams says: "If we have or are to have a culture worth treasuring, such men should be honored." He also mentions reading Rosenfeld's *Men Seen,* which would have quickened his memory of the 1920's. *Paul Rosenfeld: Voyager in the Arts,* ed. Jerome Mellquist and Lucie Wiese (New York, Creative Age Press, 1948), pp. 154-157.

44. See René Taupin, *L'Influence du Symbolisme Français sur la Poésie Américaine, de 1910 à 1920* (Paris, H. Champion, 1929), pp. 278-286, where Williams is ranked with Eliot and Pound and said to know more about the poetic imagination than any other American poet. Taupin's estimate is based on Williams' already considerable reputation in France.

45. *A Reviewer's ABC,* p. 386.

46. In defense of Pound, Eliot had said that his critical writing is "almost the only contemporary writing on the Art of Poetry that a young poet can study with profit. It forms a corpus of poetic doctrine: it has a particular relation to poetry in a particular age and it is moreover addressed primarily to the poet." The "almost" is intended to leave room for Eliot, not Williams, to whom it applies equally well. "Ezra Pound," *Poetry,* p. 331.

47. On his need for critical foundations, see *SA,* 42.

48. *SL*, 301.

49. In Chapter 16 of *GAN*, the narrator (Williams) meets Nettie, now a matron, and says, apropos Venus and Adonis, "The second time I saw her it was in a room of a hotel in the city." This is the germ of the extramarital situation of *A Dream of Love*.

50. This conjunction of Beautiful Thing and whores anticipates a theme of *Paterson V*.

51. The marriage of Williams and Flossie Herman is depicted as a new construction, an American beginning, in *The Build-Up*, which Williams wrote immediately after *The Autobiography*.

52. Pound thought that Williams looked like Cocteau. See *The Letters of Ezra Pound*, ed. D. D. Paige (New York, Harcourt, Brace and Company, 1950), p. 168. Williams may have read these letters during the composition of *The Autobiography*. This chapter on Pound, dated March 10, 1951, in the manuscript, was either the last part or among the last parts of *The Autobiography* to be written. (See Williams' manuscripts, Yale University Library.) In terms of the experience of composition it may be considered as a climax of achievement — for Williams.

53. Earlier in Part III, Williams reports a conversation with Virgil Thomson, who questioned him critically about his libretto, *The First President*. When asked, "Who is this Washington?" Williams replied: "I am Washington." (*A*, 301.) Washington is treated briefly in *IAG*; he is identified with fully in *The First President*, where he may be considered the type of the old poet.

54. The incident of the schoolteacher trying to keep her students from touching the art objects at the San Fernando Mission is an ironic comment on the Spanish conquest. His own failure to shake down the fruit of the pomegranate trees may prefigure another theme of quest, that of the hunt of the unicorn.

55. *A*, 288; see *GAN*, Chapter 13, for a boyhood memory of leaping versus yielding.

56. *A*, 174; see 343. The last episode with his grandson shows him transmitting the environment of his life (as in Whitman's "Crossing Brooklyn Ferry") to another generation. "The thing moves by a direct relationship between men from generation to generation." (*SL*, 95.)

SECTION FIVE

1. Consider this theme in *Paterson II*.

2. *Design and Truth in Autobiography* (Cambridge, Harvard University Press, 1960), p. 195.

3. Of this the anecdote of hares and hounds is representative. See *A*, 12; *VP*, 70.

4. *SL*, 53; *PB*, 169.

5. *CLP*, 260.

6. Augustine says: "So great is the force of memory, so great the force of life, even in the mortal life of man." Cited by Hans Meyerhoff, *Time in Literature* (Berkeley, University of California, 1955), p. 43. I am much indebted to this excellent study.

7. This incident was recorded on January 1, 1951, and remained unchanged in the printed version of *The Autobiography*. The last date noted on the manuscript of *The Autobiography* is March 10, 1951 (in relation to the chapter on Pound); what is presumably the first version of "The Desert Music" is dated March 11, 1951. (Williams' manuscripts, Yale University Library.)

8. *A*, 191. McAlmon's largest undertaking was Gertrude Stein's *The Making of Americans*, a book which may have influenced Williams' *White Mule* trilogy and may be compared with it.

9. *A*, 195; "The Supper," *VP*, 56-65. McAlmon's account does not mention this incident. See *Being Geniuses Together* (London, Secker and Warburg, 1938), pp. 178-184.

10. *SL*, 21.

11. *SE*, 307.

12. Emerson observed: "A poem, a sentence causes us to see ourselves. I be & I see my being, at the same time." *The Journals of Ralph Waldo Emerson,* ed. Edward Waldo Emerson and Waldo Emerson Forbes (Boston, Houghton Mifflin Company, 1909-14), IV, 180. Williams said of Shakespeare that "he went on doing the same thing all his life, over and over again, like a person who needs to reaffirm something to himself in order to keep believing it. . . ." (*SE*, 55.) And in a letter to Marianne Moore, he explained the early experience of despair which he felt had contributed to his "inner security." (*SL*, 147.)

13. The act of imagination comprises both descent (knowing one's materials) and ascent (lifting them up by ordering them); one is discovery, the other invention. In an unpublished essay, "The American Spirit in Art," he says: "Art raises the dignity of man, it allows him to say, I am, in concrete terms. It defines his environment." (Williams' manuscripts, Yale University Library.)

14. *SE*, 307-308.

15. *SE*, 14.

16. *FD*, 210.

17. See "The Artist," *PB*, 101. See also the excellent treatment of the dance in Susanne K. Langer, *Feeling and Form: A Theory of Art Developed from* Philosophy in a New Key (New York, Charles Scribner's Sons, 1953), pp. 169-207. The dance, according to Mrs. Langer, is "a play of Powers made visible" and "the creation and organization of a realm of virtual Powers." (P. 187.) Dance expresses "the consciousness of life, the sense of vital power, even of power to receive impressions, apprehend the environment, and meet changes, [which] is our most immediate self-consciousness." (P. 176.) For Williams, it is readily seen, such a conception of the dance describes the action of the imagination, its power to enter into vital contact and participate in the world and its power to create another. Dance covers what he had defined very early as the essential of poetry — "the dynamisation of emotion into a separate form" (*SA*, 67); and it answers the demand of the imagination for the satisfaction of "creative energy" (*GAN*, 330).

18. *CEP*, 169-170.

19. *The Collected Poems of Wallace Stevens* (New York, Alfred A. Knopf, 1954), p. 382.

20. In reviewing this book, Marianne Moore said of Williams: "The acknowledgement of our debt to the imagination, constitutes, perhaps, his positive value." *Contact*, No. 4 (Summer, 1921), p. 5.

21. This problem was central to the intellectual revolution of the time. In respect to the new education of the architect, Louis Sullivan tells the academically trained student that "it is with the present only that you are in physical, vital contact, and . . . real thought, vital thought, is born of the physical senses." *Kindergarten Chats and Other Writings* (New York, George Wittenborn, 1947), p. 51. Contact energizes — initiates the "dynamisation" which establishes both the poem's relation to and separateness from the world. (*SA*, 92-93.)

22. *SL*, 147.

23. *SL*, 47.

24. Thirlwall, "William Carlos Williams' 'Paterson,'" *New Directions 17*, pp. 253, 277.

25. *SA*, 1.

26. *KH*, 13.

27. The dance, to borrow Alan Ostrom's words from another context, is "the organic whole in which the natural and the human move in concert." Though Mr. Ostrom does not make this connection strongly enough, the dance is related to what

he rightly considers Williams' "central moral concern": "his concern with the propriety of all things as they exist naturally. . . ." *The Poetic World of William Carlos Williams* (Carbondale, Southern Illinois University Press, 1966), pp. 92, 68. Williams' concern with the dance also recalls Yeats's.

28. *SL*, 131.

29. The center of interest in this psychology is the relation of "organism and environment," the "orientation" of the organism and especially its "creative contact with the environment."

30. *Gestalt Therapy: Excitement and Growth in the Human Personality* (New York, Dell Publishing Company, 1965), p. viii. Originally published in 1951.

31. *CEP*, 258-259.

32. *SE*, 197; *SL*, 104; *KH, passim; SA*, 27. This dance of perception permits one, in Charles Sheeler's words, to see an object in "all of its three hundred and sixty degrees of reality"; according to Kenneth Burke, it explains how Williams, in his poems, "inordinates us into the human nature of things." See Constance Rourke, *Charles Sheeler*, p. 182; Kenneth Burke, "William Carlos Williams, 1883-1963," *William Carlos Williams: A Collection of Critical Essays*, p. 56.

33. *SE*, 72; *KH*, 59-60.

34. *SE*, 67, 71; see also *SL*, 101-102, where he tells Louis Zukofsky that "Eyes have always stood first in the poet's equipment."

35. *KH*, 69.

36. *KH*, 43.

37. *SL*, 331; *SE*, 188.

38. *SL*, 133; *CLP*, 5.

39. *A*, 89; *P*, 277.

40. *KH*, 44.

41. *PB*, 32-33. See *SE*, xvi: "Time is a storm in which we are all lost. Only inside the convolutions of the storm itself shall we find our directions — whether we measure by the latest phenomena of dada or make our computations after the archeological findings. . . ."

42. See Slate, "William Carlos Williams' Image of America," p. 90.

43. In respect to the Indian, the law also stands in the way of local realizations, the primary culture. See "The American Background," *SE*, 134-161.

44. *SE*, 188, 210, 187-188.

45. *SE*, 75; *SA*, 29, 30, 34-35; *A*, 241; Stevens, *Opus Posthumous*, p. 170.

For Williams the realism of art, its truth to nature, resides in form, and that is why measure, which determines the shape of the poem, is all important. The *actuality* of the poem is in the things composed, which Williams, like Gris, does not distort beyond recognition.

46. *SL,* 297; *A,* 241.

47. *VP,* 133. The cover design of *Kora in Hell* represents an "ovum in the act of being impregnated. . . ." (*IWW,* 28.) On the verso of page 120 of the first part of the manuscript of *The Autobiography,* Williams made a sketch of this. (Williams' manuscripts, Yale University Library.)

48. *SA,* 52-53; see also *SE,* 69-70; *P,* 258, 248; *PB,* 135-137. Addressing young writers, Williams counsels them against "inventing new ways to say 'So's your Old Man,' " and advises them to attend to the substance that forms technique and to remember that "it is a world to which we are definitely articulating — or to which we might be, were we able enough." (*SE,* 104.)

49. *PB,* 75.

50. *GAN,* 331. The river burial is also described (*IAG,* 58) in sexual terms, as Slate notes in "William Carlos Williams' Image of America," p. 124. This death, accordingly, is a seed (for survival) and Williams depicts it again, in similar terms, at the end of *Paterson IV,* where the survival of an entire culture depends upon the seeds washed into the sea of death.

51. *VP,* 126. Williams mentions his own *tactus eruditus* in *CEP,* 63; and it is possible that he is not only describing the beggar boys but projecting his own desire to touch. In his review of *IAG,* D. H. Lawrence said that there were two ways of being an American: ". . . by recoiling into individual smallness and insentience . . . the Puritan way. The other is by touch; touch America as she is; dare to touch her!" "American Heroes," *The Nation,* CXII (April 14, 1926), 413.

52. "His passion for the anti-poetic is a blood-passion etc. . . ." Preface to Williams, *Collected Poems, 1921-1931* (New York, Objectivist Press, 1934).

53. See *Paterson V*; and see also "The Three Letters," *Contact,* III (1921), 10-13, where Williams, under the name Evans Dionysius Evans, tells of his encounters with Baroness Elsa von Freytag Loringhoven and identifies her, along with his Grandmother Wellcome and Robitza of "Portrait of a Woman in Bed" (*CEP,* 150-151), as "America personified in the filth of its own imagination." Williams recalled the Baroness in *The Autobiography.*

54. *CEP,* 270-272.

55. *SL,* 156.

56. *KH,* 73. *Kora in Hell* is a mine of themes, images, and situations developed later.

57. See *CLP,* 28. There is another association: Elsie is a Jackson White and Andromeda (even though she often figures in paintings as white) is an Ethiopian princess, "dark-skinned," as Ovid says in *The Art of Love.* The old whore, therefore, may be associated with Beautiful Thing, the Negress of *Paterson III;* her "screen/of pretty doves" may remind the poet of his "dove." (*P,* 119, 152.)

58. See Northrop Frye, *Anatomy of Criticism: Four Essays* (Princeton, Princeton University Press, 1957), p. 189. In another perspective, it is Beautiful Thing, the "female principle," whom he petitions to save him in "For Eleanor and Bill Monahan." This prayer ends with the imploring words of Columbus which follow in *IAG,* 26, his wonder at "the most beautiful thing." In this late poem, they declare the poet's identification with an old defeated discoverer. (*BP,* 83-86.)

59. See my Introductory Essay to Paul Rosenfeld, *Port of New York* (Urbana, University of Illinois Press, 1961), pp. xli-xlviii. Both Crane and Williams knew this critical work, which was first published in 1924.

60. *The Bridge* in *The Collected Poems of Hart Crane,* ed. Waldo Frank (Garden City, Doubleday & Company, 1958), pp. 21-25, 45-46.

61. The significant word here is "lifts" which, for Williams, is a characteristic act of the imagination.

62. *GAN,* 329-330. This assertion does not blind Williams to the actual state of culture, which he goes on to give examples of and follows with the telling juxtaposition: "At this, De Soto, sick, after months of travel, stopped out of breath and looked about him."

63. The poem involves two examples of the dance, that of the stripper, which touches on the poet's problem and the necessity of art, and that of the American couples, with which it may be compared. The American couples may be considered as modern replicas of the giants in *Paterson* and as counterparts of the couple described in Book II:

> She stirs, distraught,
> against him — wounded (drunk), moves
> against him (a lump) desiring,
> against him, bored   .

(*P,* 75.) As such, they carry the dominant cultural theme of divorce into "The Desert Music."

64. *SA,* 54.

65. The rhythm of descent-ascent is comparable to the rhythms of death and life as Louis Sullivan understood them: "the two great forces, the simplest, elemental rhythms of Nature, to wit, the rhythm of growth, of aspiration, of that which would rise into the air: which impulse we shall call the Rhythm of Life: and the counter-rhythm of decadence, of destruction, of that which would crush to the earth, of that which makes for a return to the elements of earth, the Rhythm of Death." *Kindergarten Chats and Other Writings,* p. 121.

In another poem of this time, "Wide Awake, Full of Love," in which Williams looks "to the last" yet "will not startle for/ the grinning worm," it is the thought of love that saves him —

> . . . Your voice
> whose cello notes
> upon the theme have led
> me to the music. . . .

(*CLP,* 207.) The music of survival is also the music of love.

66. *PB,* 179.

67. See *SE,* 306:

"You are in the creative process — a function in nature — relegated to the deity.

"You have now entered what is referred to as the divine function of the artist.

". . . you are nature — in action.

"It is an action, a moving process — the verb dominates; you are to *make*."

In one version of *Paterson V,* Williams includes a long letter from Cid Corman on "The Desert Music." This letter explains how the poem introduces one, dances one into being, and how the verb underwrites the affirmative "I am." "The whole poetic act," Corman says, "is the articulation of the verb." (Williams' manuscripts, Yale University Library.)

68. *P,* 247.

69. *A,* xiii. He is referring to the unicorn tapestries. The lines on Casals in "The Desert Music" were added in a fourth or later version of the poem and were probably prompted by Williams' writing of the foreword to *The Autobiography.* See Williams' manuscripts, Yale University Library.

SECTION SIX

1. See J. Hillis Miller, *Poets of Reality: Six Twentieth-Century Writers* (Cambridge, Harvard University Press, 1965), pp. 353-355.

2. Gaston Bachelard, *The Poetics of Space* (New York, The Orion Press, 1964), p. xviii. The phrase is Pierre-Jean Jouve's. The manuscript versions of "The Desert Music" in the Yale University Library show how the very difficulty of writing this poem contributed to its theme. In version two, which goes beyond the general sketch of version one, the poet finds that he is the music and must "Retch it up," that

> I can do something
> (if I can do anything) I am a writer .

The conversation with the dinner guests is more extensive and is introduced by

> Am I William Carlos Williams,
> the poet? Am I   . ?
> whose head is split open
> so that poems drop, out?

And the poet later affirms his vocation in the margin ("I am a poet! I am") alongside this statement in the text:

> I know I am a poet having failed [?]
> the poet

As he had in the composition of *Paterson,* Williams successively elaborated his original materials and extracted the poem from them. In doing this his primary object was to make a dramatic and active form out of expository and passive materials, and it is significant that in version two, where the idea of self-realization becomes prominent, he speaks of writing plays, not poems, as a way of expressing himself. (In the published poem he becomes an actor on the stage of memory.)

This method of composition almost invariably improved the original scenario, the only loss being an occasional obscurity due to the excision of "explanatory" material. The poem, of course, is adequate in itself; my own reading of it was made before I consulted the manuscripts. But the manuscripts themselves are a part of the drama of the poem and should be worked through as part of the reading of the poem — for the sake of the sometimes prosaic clarity (and confirmation) of the original material and for a just sense of the many transformations and realizations achieved by Williams' art.

It is also instructive to note the poet's experiments with the format of the poem in its several published versions. By indenting sections of verse, Williams tried to indicate present and past, and perhaps the depth, or importance to self, of a passage, as in the final quatrain. In the text of the poem in *Pictures from Brueghel,* the narrated incident ("The Old Market" and what follows) is set in from what precedes it and the comment about the Indians' nauseating prattle is also lined up to show that it occurs within this experience. The only lapses from this are the passages beginning "There is another music" and "Old fashioneds all around?" which are set as far left as the verse at the beginning of the poem and, to keep the scheme, should be indented.

3. *VP*, 132.

4. *CEP*, 243.

5. *P*, 167. On p. 162 he writes,

> But somehow a man must lift himself
> again —
>> again is the magic word

6. *CEP*, 460.

7. *P*, 167.

8. *CEP*, 25.

9. *PB*, 67.

10. Edward Dahlberg, *Alms for Oblivion* (Minneapolis, The University of Minnesota Press, 1964), p. 46; see also Williams' foreword to Robert E. Knoll, *Robert McAlmon: Expatriate Publisher and Writer* (Lincoln, The University of Nebraska Press, 1959).

11. *CLP*, 106.

12. *VP*, 237.

13. *PB*, 164.

14. "W.C.W.: An Italian View," *Prairie Schooner*, p. 314.

15. See *CEP*, 78; *SE*, 241-249.

16. *ML*, 213.

17. *PB*, 179.

18. *P*, 273. The pun above is Thoreau's. See *The Writings of Henry David Thoreau, Journal*, II, 204, for a relevant discussion of the relation of the mind to "the primal womb of things."

19. Wordsworth, Preface to *Lyrical Ballads*; Thoreau, "The Succession of Forest Trees."

20. *CLP*, 260; *A*, 328. See also Thoreau on hope-bearing seeds, in the concluding paragraph of "The Bean-Field," *Walden*.

21. *SA*, 43.

22. *PB*, 180; Thirlwall, "William Carlos Williams as Correspondent," *The Literary Review*, p. 19.

23. *SL*, 296-297.

24. *CEP*, 229.

25. *Briarcliff Quarterly*, 207.

26. Ezra Pound, *Selected Poems* (London, Faber & Gwyer,

1928), pp. x-xi. Williams wrote appreciatively of Pound's contribution to measure in an incompleted essay, dated January 13, 1950. See "The Later Pound," Williams' manuscripts, Yale University Library.

27. Inventions are forms for our functions (*SE,* 178-179); they test the poet, as in the case of Sandburg, whose poems "technically . . . reveal no initiative. . . ." (*SE,* 272.) Williams was always, and increasingly, concerned with invention, and in *Paterson V* celebrates, as Roy Harvey Pearce says, "the power of invention itself." *The Continuity of American Poetry* (Princeton, Princeton University Press, 1961), p. 348.

28. *GAN,* 334.

29. *PB,* 95-96.

30. F. R. Leavis, *New Bearings in English Poetry: A Study of the Contemporary Situation* (London, Chatto and Windus Ltd., 1932), pp. 25, 26, 18, 24. The test derives from Eliot: see introduction to Pound, *Selected Poems,* pp. xx-xxi. The situation in English poetry in 1932 is suggested by the fact that two Americans, Pound and Eliot, are chiefly responsible for it; Williams, who, with Pound and Eliot, was prominent in René Taupin's study, is not mentioned by Leavis.

The concluding phrase is from *SL,* 297.

:: index

Burke, Kenneth, 113, 114, 121, 128

Caetani, Princess Marguerite, 15
Carnevali, Emanuel, 54; *A Hurried Man*, 40
Casals, Pablo, 94, 97, 102, 131
Charles Sheeler: Artist in the American Tradition (Rourke), 122
"Clarity," 20, 21, 22
Cloisters, The, 97
Cocteau, Jean, 125
Columbus, Christopher, 18, 26, 52, 53, 86, 100, 114, 130
Contact, 53, 65
Contact, 30, 38, 71-72, 74, 78, 85, 92, 93, 121, 127, 129
Corman, Cid, 131
Crane, Hart, 130; *The Bridge*, 32, 88, 90
"Crossing Brooklyn Ferry" (Whitman), 125
Culture, 30-31, 41, 49, 60, 105, 115-116, 117-118, 121, 124, 130; poet of, 31, 32-33, 34-35, 38, 39, 43, 61, 90, 99, 108, 116, 119

Dance, 20, 26, 68-76, 81, 82, 86, 89, 91, 96, 98, 127, 128
Death, 28-29, 36, 39, 42, 43, 46, 60, 62, 63, 69, 77, 81, 95-96, 100, 102, 103-104, 105, 106-107, 129
Descent, 17, 21-24, 63-64, 67, 68, 69, 71, 78, 95, 97, 101, 114, 122, 126, 131. *See also* Ascent
De Soto, Hernando, 83-84, 86, 130
Dewey, John, 22, 31, 72
Dickey, James, 119
Dickinson, Emily, 36
Dillon, George, 33
Discovery, 4, 20, 53, 57, 83, 126
Donoghue, Denis, 116
Dryden, John, 56

Egoist, The, 21
Einstein, Albert, 115
Eliot, T. S., ix, xi, 29, 30, 31, 32, 33, 44, 49, 61, 65, 66, 106, 108, 109, 115, 116, 117, 119, 120, 124, 134; *Four Quartets*, 37, 57; introduction to Pound, *Selected Poems*, 108; *The Sacred Wood*, 66; *The Use of Poetry and the Use of Criticism*, xi, 121; *The Waste Land*, 35, 54, 106, 124
Emerson, Ralph Waldo, 26, 80, 126
Expatriation, 21, 29, 33, 35, 57, 108

Fall of Hyperion, The (Keats), 114-115